Family or Foe

A Case of a Severe Personality Disorder

JEWEL GARRISON

authorHOUSE®

AuthorHouse™ UK
1663 Liberty Drive
Bloomington, IN 47403 USA
www.authorhouse.co.uk
Phone: 0800.197.4150

Published by AuthorHouse   06/21/2017

ISBN: 978-1-5246-8100-5 (sc)
ISBN: 978-1-5246-8101-2 (hc)
ISBN: 978-1-5246-8103-6 (e)

Print information available on the last page.

Any people depicted in stock imagery provided by Thinkstock are models,
and such images are being used for illustrative purposes only.
Certain stock imagery © Thinkstock.

This book is printed on acid-free paper.

Contents

READERS' VIEWS AND FEEDBACK

"Your case study, and more broadly the intricacies of personality disorders, appears really quite interesting. The subject is highly topical, and I would imagine that while providing keen insight into the matter this study would also offer some personal, emotional appeal. .... looks very interesting. This strikes me as the type of book that would offer fantastic supplementary reading for students". by Tom.Payne@mheducation.com (editor McGraw Hill)

"Thank you very much for sending your manuscript. .... it certainly made an interesting read and is well researched". by Ruth Chalmers; ruthc@pavpub.com

This book is dedicated to the late Elsie Fynba Clarke, my beloved mother, whose sacrifices have brought me thus far. I am indelibly grateful for her altruism that laid the foundation for my achievements.

Acknowledgements

Special thanks to my children, Maximillian, Michael, and Myles, who have always been there for me from their childhood. They have been my backbone throughout my studies and career development over the years, through thick and thin, and I am grateful for their unfailing support, patience, tolerance, and encouragement and sincerely apologise for inconveniences caused to them during their growing up because of my determination.

Special thanks to Professor Isaac Galyuon, Dr Michael Tettey, and Professor Joseph Aggrey-Fynn of the University of Cape Coast in Ghana for their ongoing support in all my endeavours.

Thanks to my siblings, Alethea, Eunice, and Vida, and all the members of the extended family whose collaboration and corroboration contributed immensely to this study.

Special thanks to my nephews, Akakyi and Ben, whose help and assistance around my home enabled me to continue with my background research for this study.

Abstract

Personality disorder is rife in Ghana, but the people of Ghana are totally oblivious to this fact, and for this reason many peoples' behaviours leave me to suspect that they may be suffering from severe personality disorders. In the absence of any knowledge about mental illness, the public does not appear to know what this disorder is or constitutes; neither do they understand the implications of someone having the disorder or having to live with someone with the disorder.

Because of the stigma attached to mental illness, the people of Ghana are in denial of their mental health status, and as such do not accept that anyone could be mentally ill. Even those affected and their families do not wish to broach the issue and so would prefer to attend prayer camps and other unhygienic places in seeking help and treatment, believing they have been afflicted by some form of a superstitious order rather than a mental illness.

This is a case study of a man who, by all accounts, has a personality disorder of the schizotypal, paranoid, schizoid, histrionic, antisocial, borderline, and narcissistic types, but who no one knows about because of the lack of awareness and knowledge about the subject of mental health. For anonymity, I shall refer to this man as Tamzin.

Is the damage caused by the personality disorder beyond repair and is it too late for Tamzin to get help? These two concerns are addressed by this case study.

The case study reviews the theories and literature underpinning personality and personality disorders respectively to make a case for a diagnosis of a personality disorder. It also highlights gaps in the mental health service and provision in Ghana, as well as the implications to policy, practice, education, and research of a person living in the community with a personality disorder, offering some recommendations for the way forward in the same areas as those for implications.

Aim

To explore the concept of personality disorder to determine its prevalence in and gain insight into Tamzin's state of mind to determine whether he has a personality disorder and to explore the feasibility of treating his disorder considering the absence of appropriate service.

Objectives

- To critically analyse the evidence underpinning personality theories
- To explore and determine whether Tamzin has a personality disorder
- To identify what disorder and which theory may be at play
- To establish what went wrong with Tamzin that led to his disorder
- To draw out the implications of this case study to health care and provision in Ghana
- To make recommendations for the way forward as highlighted by this case study

Chapter One

Introduction

In the case I am about to narrate, the individual has come to the attention of the police through instances of disorderly conduct and behaviours like drunkenness, physical altercation, verbal altercation, and vandalism, yet at no point in time was his mental health even considered; neither was he considered for referral to the psychiatric service for the examination of his mental state.

This is about a man living within the extended family making a name for himself by creating the impression that he is a hero, Mr Fix-It, and jack of all trade, but in fact he is manipulating the members of the family, creating rifts between family members, splitting his siblings and the extended family members, vandalizing their properties, and turning around to fix and repair the damages to show how good he is, all under the guise of Mr Nice Man.

The case study will explore the challenges in witnessing the signs that indicate that the individual concerned is suffering from, though he has not been formally diagnosed with, a personality disorder though he has come to the attention of the police on several occasions.

On reflection, however, by applying my knowledge and experiences in psychology and psychiatry as well as community psychiatric nursing, I can now appreciate his difficulties and probably his pain, which he is too proud to admit to and/or to self-disclose. I suspect he has some insight but is either too embarrassed to acknowledge he has a mental health problem or, possibly, is genuinely totally oblivious to his disposition since both Ghana and Nigeria, where he emigrated to, are in denial of the mental health issues engulfing their populations because of the stigma attached to mental illness, although whether he is mentally ill or not is yet to be proven.

To make a case for personality disorder manifesting in Tamzin's mental state, I shall need to, firstly, define personality and describe the theories of personality, looking at the underpinning themes and, critically, at their strengths, weaknesses, and what the critics have to say about them. Describing all the theories involved in issues of personality will be beyond the scope of this book, and therefore I will focus only on the salient and pertinent perspectives of the five main theories.

I will critically analyse the evidence underpinning personality theories, explore and determine whether this man I refer to as Tamzin for this book has a personality disorder of some sort, and identify, if present, what disorder he has and which theory could be the culprit. I will endeavour to explore and establish what went wrong, looking at issues of childhood, abuse, parental marital discord and subsequent breakup, displacement of children when the marriage broke up, and migration. I will look at challenges Tamzin encountered and how having to deal with the challenges has taken its toll on him. I shall conclude with a discussion of the issues highlighted and the way forward, asking the question whether it is too late to rescue Tamzin and how and whether he wants to be rescued at all.

First, we must begin by answering the most basic question: What is personality?

Chapter Two

What Is Personality?

The concept of personality appears deceptively simple, but in fact it is very complex. Historically, the term *personality* was derived from the Greek *persona*, which was the theatrical mask used by dramatic players (Boyd, 2005). Originally, the term had the connotation of a projected pretence, make-believe, or illusion (Boyd, 2005). With time, the connotation changed from an external surface representation to the internal traits of the individual (Boyd, 2005).

Personality is a complex pattern of characteristics, largely outside of the person's awareness, that comprises the individual's distinctive pattern of perceiving, feeling, thinking, coping, and behaving (Millon and Davis, 1999). And it emerges from a complicated interaction of biologic dispositions, psychological experiences, and environmental situations (Millon and Davis, 1999). It is a dynamic and organized set of characteristics possessed by a person that uniquely influences his or her environment, cognitions, emotions, motivations, and behavioural science in various situations (Millon and Davis, 1999).

Research in this area is driven by observation and or experience rather than theory or pure logic, such as dimensional models, based on multivariate statistics, such as factor analysis, or emphasizes theory development, such as that of the psychodynamic theory. (Roychowdhury and Adshead 2014).

There is also a substantial emphasis on the applied field of personality testing. In psychological education and training, the study of the nature of personality and its psychological development is usually reviewed as a prerequisite to courses in abnormal or clinical psychology (Roychowdhury and Adshead 2014).

Gordon Allport (1937) gave two modes of how to study personality: the nomothetic and the idiographic. Idiographic psychology applies general laws to several different people, such as the principle of self-actualization. Idiographic psychology is an attempt to understand the unique aspects of an individual (Allport, 1937).

It doesn't appear that we have a conclusive definition of *personality* in psychology. Allport asserted, "Personality is the dynamic organization within the individual of those psychophysical systems that determine his characteristics, behaviour and thought" (Allport, 1961). And Weinberg and Gould maintained that personality is "the characteristics or blend of characteristics that make a person unique" (Weinberg and Gould, 1999). Both definitions emphasize the uniqueness of the individual and consequently adopt an idiographic view.

Personality also describes the individual's mode of thinking and feeling, as well as how they comport themselves in public in a consistent fashion time and time again that distinguishes them from others in terms of self-perceptions, values, and attitudes as well as predicting their reactions to other people, problems, and stress.

Today, personality is conceptualized as a complex pattern of psychological characteristics that are not easily altered and that are largely outside of the person's awareness (Millon and Davis, 1999). These characteristics or traits include the individual's specific style of perceiving, thinking, and feeling about self, others, and the environment (Millon and Davis, 1999). These styles or traits are similar across many different social or personal situations and are expressed in almost every facet of functioning (Millon and Davis, 1999). Intrinsic and pervasive, they emerge from a complicated interaction of biologic dispositions, environmental situations and psychological experiences, that ultimately comprise the individual's distinctive personality (Millon and Davis, 1999).

Philosophical Assumptions

Strictly speaking, the study of personality is not purely an empirical discipline since it involves elements of art, science, and philosophy to arrive at general conclusions (Engler, 2008). Many of the ideas applied by theorists originate from the basic philosophical assumptions that they each hold, and the following brief descriptions highlight the five categories of the most fundamental philosophical assumptions that theorists disagree on (Engler, 2008).

Freedom versus Determinism: This assumption questions what control we have over our behaviour: is behaviour determined causally by forces beyond our control, or do we have control over our behaviour and understand the motives behind our behaviour (Engler, 2008)? The behaviour is classed as unconscious, environmental, or biological by many theorists (Engler, 2008).

Heredity versus Environment: Here, personality is presumed to be either genetically and biologically or environmentally and experientially determined (Engler, 2008).

Uniqueness versus Universality: This assumption discusses the human individuality in terms of his or her uniqueness or similarity in nature in terms of universality (Engler, 2008). Gordon Allport, Abraham Maslow, and Carl Rogers embraced the idea of individuals being unique (Engler, 2008). Behaviourists and theorists of cognition, on the other hand, are firm about how important reinforcement and self-efficacy principles are (Engler, 2008).

Active versus Reactive: Here the assumption explores using our initiative as being active or coming from an outside stimulus as in reacting; behaviourists traditionally assert that the environment shapes the individuals who are passive and don't participate in their shaping, whilst the theorists from the humanistic and cognitive perspectives are in consensus about individuals partaking in their duties (Engler, 2008). Most modern theorists agree that both contribute to our behaviour with most of how we behave being brought to bear by traits, and the main predictor of individual's behaviour in the short term brought about by situations (Fleeson, 2004; Zayas and Shoda, 2009; Tapu, 2001).

Optimism versus Pessimism: Here the theories disagree on whether we remain part and parcel in how our own personalities change (Engler, 2008); the theories that stress the need for learning are more hopeful than the ones that do not (Engler, 2008).

Chapter Three

Personality Theories Literature Review

Full descriptions of all the theories are beyond the scope of this book, so only the pertinent perspectives of the five main theories will be succinctly described.

Behavioural Theories

Behavioural theories suggest that personality is a result of interaction between the individual and the environment (Cheney and Pierce, 2008; Mischel, 1993) they explain personality as how outside stimulus affects behaviour (Cheney and Pierce, 2008). This way of thinking was a major change from the Freudian way of thinking. One of the biggest principles of these psychology theorists is a stress on a scientific way of thinking and carrying out experiments (Mischel, 1993). This style of thinking was started by B. F. Skinner (Cheney and Pierce, 2008; Mischel, 1993), who asserted that there is a mutual relationship between the person or "the organism" with its environment (Cheney and Pierce, 2008; Mischel, 1993). According to Skinner's way of thinking, behaviour is brought about by events, such as operant conditioning (Cheney and Pierce, 2008; Mischel, 1993). Ivan Pavlov is another popular influence who is well known for his classical conditioning experiments involving dogs, which led him to discover the foundation of behaviourism (Cheney and Pierce, 2008).

Although it is believed that genes supply many ways for different cells to present, the environment decides which of these manifest, according to behaviourists (Cheney and Pierce, 2008). They posit that interactions between the environment and DNA are crucial in the makings of personality (Cheney and Pierce, 2008) because this relationship brings about which part of the DNA code is turned into proteins that will become part of the individual (Cheney and Pierce, 2008). Behaviourists assert that, while the genome provides different choices, in the end, it is the environment that decides what manifests (Cheney and Pierce, 2008). Behavioural theorists study observable and measurable behaviours, rejecting theories that take internal thoughts and feelings into account (Cheney and Pierce, 2008). Corr (2007) cites research inspired by Eysenck's theories that confirm that personality is not an entity separate from brain-behavioural processes but is, in fact, defined by them.

Biological Theories

The biological basis of personality is the theory that personality is influenced by the biology of the brain (Plomin, DeFries, et al., 1997; Damasio, Grabowski, et al., 1994). Biology, it is suggested, is instrumental in the development of personality (Eysenck, 1952), with biological approaches suggesting that genetics are responsible for personality (Plomin, DeFries, et al., 1997; Damasio, Grabowski, et al., 1994). Therefore, the study of the involvement of biology in personality psychology seeks first to find out what part the genes play and how these shape individual personalities (Plomin, DeFries, et al., 1997; Damasio, Grabowski, et al., 1994). Many of the earliest thinking about possible biological underpinnings of personality emerged from the case of Phineas Gage (Damasio, Grabowski, et al., 1994). In an 1848 accident, a large iron rod was reported to have been driven through the head of an individual called Gage, which apparently changed his personality, although the form (Damasio, Grabowski, et al., 1994) of these psychological changes is noted to be usually exaggerated (Macmillan, 2000; Macmillan, 2008). To confirm this evidence, it has not been easy to find patients with brain injury to study. In the 1990s, researchers used electroencephalography (EEG), positron emission tomography (PET), and presently functional magnetic resonance imaging (fMRI), which is now the most widely used imaging technique, to help localize personality traits in the brain (Macmillan, 2000; Macmillan, 2008).

The Neurotransmitters Involvement: Dopamine and Serotonin Pathways

The biology-based personality theories are based on correlating personality traits (Plomin, DeFries, et al., 1997; Damasio, Grabowski, et al., 1994) with behavioural systems related to motivation, reward, and punishment (Plomin, DeFries, et al., 1997). On a broad level, this involves the autonomic nervous system (Plomin, DeFries, et al., 1997; Damasio, Grabowski, et al., 1994), fear-processing circuits in the amygdala (Plomin, DeFries, et al., 1997; Damasio, Grabowski, et al., 1994), the reward pathway from the ventral tegmental area (VTA) (Plomin, DeFries, et al., 1997; Damasio, Grabowski, et al., 1994) to the nucleus accumbens (Plomin, DeFries, et al., 1997; Damasio, Grabowski, et al., 1994), and prefrontal cortex (Plomin, DeFries, et al., 1997; Damasio, Grabowski, et al., 1994). These circuits heavily rely on neurotransmitters and their precursors, yet the most research support is for dopamine and serotonin pathways (Plomin, DeFries, et al., 1997; Damasio, Grabowski, et al., 1994).

Dopamine is a monoamine neurotransmitter that has been found to promote exploratory behaviour (Terracciano, Antonio, et al., 2009). Dopaminergic pathways have been specifically correlated with the extraversion trait of the five-factor model of personality (Terracciano, Antonio, et al., 2009). The monoamine oxidase (MAO) enzyme has a preferential affinity for dopamine and is correlated with sensation seeking (Terracciano, Antonio, et al., 2009).

Serotonin is a monoamine neurotransmitter and has been found to promote avoidance behaviour through inhibitory pathways (Terracciano, Antonio, et al., 2009); specifically, serotonin has been associated with neuroticism, agreeableness, and conscientiousness (traits defined by the five-factor model of personality) (Terracciano, Antonio, et al., 2009).

One of the best-known biological theorists was Hans Eysenck, who linked aspects of personality to biological processes. For example, Eysenck argued that introverts have high cortical arousal, leading them to avoid stimulation. Eysenck believed, on the other hand, that extroverts have low cortical arousal, causing them to seek out stimulating experiences.

Genetic Involvement in Development of Personality

Research on heritability suggests that there is a link between genetics and personality traits. The human genome is known to play a part in the development of personality. Ever since the Human Genome Project gave the light for a much more detailed comprehension of genes, (Gazzaniga and Heatherton, 2006) there has been a continuum of debates on the involvement of how the individual inherits personality traits, and the way the environment affects personality versus how the genes affect personality (Allport,1937; Skinner,1984b; Damasio and Grabowski, et al., 1994). Previously, studies on genetic personality were more interested in specific genes correlating to specific personality traits. Today's view of the interaction between the genes shows more interest in the activation and expression of genes related to personality and forms part of what is referred to as behavioural genetics. Several studies have reported an interaction in several different ways of how our bodies can develop, but the interaction between the genes and the shaping of our minds and personality is also relevant to this interaction between genes (Gazzaniga and Heatherton, 2006). Minor changes in DNA in individuals distinguishes them from each other as well as the differences in the way they look, their abilities, how their brains function, and all the features that make up the development of a cohesive personality (Marcus, 2004). Cattell (1965) and Eysenck (1982) proposed that genetics are strongly instrumental in the development of our personality with a huge part of the evidence that associates genes and the environment in the making of a personality coming from twin studies (Loehlin and Nicholas, 1976). This "twin method" focused on how similar the twins were in personality using genetically identical twins (Loehlin and Nicholas, 1976). One of the earliest twin studies measured 800 pairs of twins, studied numerous personality traits, and determined that identical twins are most similar in their general abilities (Loehlin and Nicholas, 1976). Personality similarities were found to be less related for self-concepts, goals, and interests (Loehlin and Nicholas, 1976).

Humanist Theories

The humanistic perspective focuses on the positive image of humans (McLeod, 2007); the humanistic evaluation of personality is based around positive attitude (Lahey, 2009; McLeod, 2007), which will cause a person to fulfil his or her full potential (Lahey, 2009; McLeod, 2007). In the humanistic perspective, humans are considered basically good (Lahey, 2009; McLeod, 2007) and are hopeful of fulfilling their full potential (Lahey, 2009; McLeod, 2007). They emphasize the conscious awareness of needs, choices, and personal responsibility of the individual (Lahey, 2009). The humanistic perspective expects people to be upbeat and positive (Lahey, 2009), which will help them attain their potential; this humanistic perspective believes that when people understand who they are, they can be happier because they can fulfil their potential and become more satisfied in life (Lahey, 2009; McLeod, 2007; Watt and Norman, 1981). Humanistic theories emphasize the importance of free will and individual experience in the development of personality as well as the concept of self-actualization (Lahey, 2009; McLeod, 2007), which is an innate need for personal growth that motivates behaviour (Lahey, 2009; McLeod, 2007). These theories focus on subjective experiences of individuals as opposed to forced, definitive factors that determine behaviour (Combs and Snygg, 1949), and the theorists include Carl Rogers and Abraham Maslow (Combs and Snygg, 1949). Maslow and Rogers viewed the individual as partaking in what goes on in his environment responding appropriately to perceptions and encounters (Maslow, 1999). They viewed humanistic theories as positive and optimistic proposals (Lahey, 2009; McLeod, 2007) that stress the individual making attempts to develop and grow without prompting (Watt and Norman, 1981). This motivation is the centre of the individual's progress in life and makes him who he is (Combs and Snygg, 1949; Maslow, 1999).

Psychodynamic Theories

Psychodynamic theories of personality are heavily influenced by the work of Sigmund Freud. They emphasize the influence of the unconscious mind and childhood experiences on personality. Psychodynamic theories include Sigmund Freud's psychosexual stage theory and Erik Erikson's stages of psychosocial development. Erikson believed that personality progresses through a series of stages, with certain conflicts arising at each stage. Success in any stage depended upon successfully overcoming preceding conflicts.

Freud copied the term *thermodynamics* to coin the term *psychodynamics* (Kahn, 2002). Based on the idea of converting heat into mechanical energy, he asserted that psychic energy could be converted into behaviour (Kahn, 2002). Freud's theory emphasizes dynamic, unconscious psychological conflicts (Kahn, 2002) and divides the human personality into three significant components: the id, the ego, and the super-ego (Carver and Scheier, 2004). The id responds to the "pleasure principle", which focuses on immediate gratification of its needs regardless of the situation (Carver and Scheier, 2004). The ego then emerges to realistically meet the wishes and demands of the id in accordance with the outside world, adhering to the "reality principle" (Carver and Scheier, 2004). Finally, the superego (conscience) compels the ego to act morally according to societal rules (Carver and Scheier, 2004), thus forcing the ego to meet the demands of the id realistically as well as (Carver and Scheier, 2004) morally (Carver and Scheier, 2004), the superego being the last function of the personality to develop (Carver and Scheier, 2004) and the embodiment of parental/social ideals established during childhood (Carver and Scheier, 2004). According to Freud, personality is based on the dynamic interactions of these three components (Carver and Scheier, 2004).

Trait Theories

The trait theory approach is one of the largest areas within personality psychology (McAdams, 2009). According to this theory, personality is made up of elements of broad traits (Aluja, Garcia, and Garcia, 2004). A trait is basically a relatively stable characteristic that causes an individual to behave in certain ways (Feist and Gregory, 2009). Some of the best-known trait theories include Eysenck's three-dimension theory (Eysenck, 1952; 66) and the five-factor theory of personality (Aluja, Garcia, and Garcia, 2004).

According to the *Diagnostic and Statistical Manual* (DSM-IV-TR) of the American Psychiatric Association (2000), personality traits are "enduring patterns of perceiving, relating to, and thinking about the environment and oneself that are exhibited in a wide range of social and personal contexts." Theorists generally assume that:

- Traits are relatively stable over time (Allport, 1937; Cattell, 1965; Eysenck, 1952).
- Traits differ among individuals (Allport, 1937; Cattell, 1965; Eysenck, 1952).

- Traits influence behaviour (Allport, 1937; Cattell, 1965; Eysenck, 1952).

These are used consistently to define an individual (Feist and Gregory, 2009).

Traits are also bipolar and vary along a continuum between one extreme and the other; e.g., friendly versus unfriendly (Feist and Gregory, 2009).

The most common models of traits incorporate three to five broad dimensions or factors (Aluja, Garcia, and Garcia, 2004). All trait-related theories include at least two features or measures, namely, extraversion and neuroticism, which first came to light through the humoral theory of Hippocrates (Aluja, Garcia, and Garcia, 2004). Gordon Allport (1937) described various types of traits, which he also referred to as dispositions (McAdams, 2009). Basic individual personality is known as a central trait, while a secondary trait is not so important as the central (McAdams, 2009). Traits that are common within a culture (cultural traits) vary from culture to culture (McAdams, 2009). Cardinal traits are those by which an individual may be strongly recognized (McAdams, 2009). In his book, *Personality: A Psychological Interpretation*, Gordon Allport (1937) both established personality psychology as a legitimate intellectual discipline and introduced the first of the modern trait theories (McAdams, 2009).

Raymond Cattell's research propagated a two-tiered personality structure with sixteen "primary factors" and developed the Sixteen Personality Factor Questionnaire (Cattell, 1965). He also identified five "secondary factors" (Cattell, 1965) and defined personality as "that which permits a prediction of what a person will do in any given situation" (Cattell, 1965). Hans Eysenck, on the other hand, believed that just three traits, namely, extraversion, neuroticism, and psychoticism, would do to distinguish between human personalities (Eysenck, 1952).

Critical Analysis of the Evidence Underpinning Personality Theories

A full critique of all the theories is beyond the scope of this book, so I shall focus on the five main theories with a succinct critical analysis of their salient perspectives only.

Behavioural Theories

Although most theories make assumptions about humans having some sort of a free will and being moral thinkers (Mischel, 1993), behaviourists refuse to acknowledge the innate workings of individuals (Mischel, 1993; Skinner, 1993). The behaviourist views humans as nothing short of mediators between behaviour and the environment (Skinner, 1993) dismissing the impact or involvement of biological and social factors on humans (Mischel, 1993). It is suggested, however, that heredity and environment interact to determine one's personality and not just environment alone (Goldberg, 1990; Jeronimus, Riese et al., 2014), while Corr (2007) cites research inspired by Eysenck's theories, which confirms that personality is not an entity separate from brain-behavioural processes, but is in fact defined by them.

The lack of acknowledgement of the innate workings of individuals is the one major problem opponents have with the behavioural theory and this, alongside its inability to explain the human phenomenon of language and memory, is a major setback against behavioural theory, rendering it incomprehensible. Critics, however, admit to behavioural theory and its ideology having a lot to contribute towards certain behaviours expressed by the individual.

Thorndike's Law of Effect

Although the evidence was present, E. L. Thorndike did not believe that classical conditioning was comprehensive since Pavlov's theory could not be explained because most behaviours in the natural environment were not simple enough (Schwartz and Lacy, 1982).

Positive and Negative Reinforcement – B. F. Skinner

Though Thorndike developed the basic law of effect (Schwartz and Lacy, 1982), Skinner took it and constructed a research programme on the experiments he had conducted in his study around it basing it on punishment and reward (Mischel, 1993). Skinner asserted that the behaviour caused by the law of effect would be called operant conditioning (Mischel, 1993) because the behaviour of an organism changed or operated in the environment (Mischel, 1993). There were no real environmental stimuli forcing a response from an organism as in classical conditioning (Mischel, 1993). Operant conditioning consists of two important elements, the operant or response (Mischel, 1993) and the consequence (Mischel, 1993). If the consequence is favourable or positively reinforcing, then the likelihood of another similar response is more than if the consequence is punishing (Mischel, 1993).

The Natural Selection Theory by Darwin: Contradictions with the Ideas

Despite Darwin's theory being widely accepted by most scientists, behavioural theory is frequently under scrutiny by critics (Dahlbom, 1984). It is for this reason that B. F. Skinner chooses to form an alliance with Darwin's theory to gain credibility for his own theory (Dahlbom, 1984), but as Dahlbom (1984) points out, Skinner's operant conditioning theory is contradicted by some ideas in Darwin's theory, such as the fact that humans are constantly improving themselves to achieve better self-control: "To increase self-control means to increase liberty" (Dahlbom, 1984) or free-will. This is a point Skinner's theory dismisses (Dahlbom, 1984). The very basis on which Skinner formed his theory is, thus, a direct contradiction of Darwin's ideas and, therefore, flawed (Dahlbom, 1984).

Also, according to Wyrwicka (1984), Skinner compares the positive reinforcement drive inherent in his operant conditioning with proposal of the natural selection drive in nature, by Darwin, but the natural selection drive is dependent on what is necessary for the survival of the species, and "the consequences of operant behaviour are not so much survival as sensory gratification" (Wyrwicka, 1984). Given that what is most pleasurable to the senses is not always what is best for the survival of an individual's genes, (Wyrwicka, 1984), very often these two drives contradict one another (Wyrwicka, 1984). For instance, inhaling cocaine and indulging in dangerous sports are two popular lifestyles despite the hazards they pose to one's life (Wyrwicka, 1984). Darwin's ideas are more acceptable than operant conditioning (Wyrwicka, 1984); by contradicting Darwin's ideas, Skinner's operant conditioning theory loses much of its support, something Skinner had hoped to achieve by his parallels (Wyrwicka, 1984).

Generalization of Behaviourist Findings in Humans

All or most of all the experiments carried out by behaviourists involved the use of animals such as Pavlov's classical conditioning and Skinner's operant conditioning and the findings generalized to humans. How appropriate is this concept? Boulding (1984) questions Skinner's application of the findings of animal behaviour studies to humans, thus implying that laws relating to lower animals' behaviour can be generalized in the complex human behaviours. Since this assumption has not yet been proven accurate and relevant in humans, it is no wonder that the basis upon which the behaviourist theories lie remains unfounded, and therefore, to ensure validity of behaviourist theories, it is essential that human participants are used (Boulding, 1984). It is also unethical to assume that what works for animals will necessarily apply in humans despite there being complex processes involved in human behaviours.

Although it is believed that genes supply many ways for different cells to present, the environment, however, decides which of these manifest, according to behaviourists (Cheney and Pierce, 2008). They posit that interactions between the environment and DNA are crucial in the makings of personality (Cheney and Pierce, 2008) because this relationship brings about what part of the DNA code gets turned into proteins that will become part of the individual (Cheney and Pierce, 2008).

Biological Theories

The biological personality theories previously discussed, on a broad level, involve the autonomic nervous system, fear-processing circuits in the amygdala (Plomin, DeFries, et al., 1997; Damasio, Grabowski, et al., 1994), the reward pathway from the ventral tegmental area (VTA) (Plomin, DeFries, et al., 1997; Damasio, Grabowski et al., 1994) to the nucleus accumbens (Plomin, DeFries, et al, 1997; Damasio, Grabowski, et al., 1994), and prefrontal cortex (Plomin, DeFries, et al, 1997; Damasio, Grabowski, et al., 1994), all of which circuits heavily rely on neurotransmitters and their precursors, but have not been heavily and seriously investigated like the dopamine and serotonin pathways (Terracciano, Antonio, et al., 2009).

Twin Studies

Twin studies have also been important in the creation of the five-factor personality model: neuroticism, extraversion, openness, agreeableness, and conscientiousness; neuroticism and extraversion (Loehlin and Nicholas, 1976) being the two most widely studied traits. One study measuring genetic influence on twins in five different countries found that the correlations for identical twins were .50, while for fraternal they were about .20 (Loehlin and Nicholas, 1976). It is suggested that heredity and environment interact to determine one's personality and not heredity alone (Goldberg, 1990; Jeronimus, Riese, et al., 2014).

Experiments to Determine Personality

There are many techniques for measuring the biology of the brain by experiments, but five main methods are mostly applied to investigate the biological involvement of personality (DeYoung, 2010). The data collected are mainly correlated with traits personality, which is often determined by personality questionnaires that may be biased because they are self-reporting and therefore unreliable. Scientists therefore emphasize the use of other different measures of personality (DeYoung, 2010; Zukerman, 2006) rather than the sole self-reported questionnaires normally used.

Some of the biological basis for personality grew out of the case of Phineas Gage, but it has not been possible to validate this because it is difficult to find patients with brain damage to study (Damasio, Grabowski, et al., 1994), and even the psychological changes described in the case of Phineas Gage have been known to be exaggerated (Macmillan, 2000; Macmillan, 2008) as previously mentioned.

Nature versus Nurture

This is another question that may someday be answerable: To what degree is who we are due to our genetic inheritance ("nature") or to our upbringing and other experiences ("nurture")? The question is such a difficult one because nature and nurture do not exist independently of each other. Both body and experience are probably essential to being a person, and it is very difficult to separate their effects. This issue comes up in many forms, including the possible existence of instincts in human beings and the nature of temperament, as well as genetically based personality characteristics. It is also very debatable whether "nature" (as in human nature) even refers to genetics.

Humanist Theories

Judgements applied in humanistic theory are said to be subjective as they allow the individual judging to decide or determine someone's potential (Lahey, 2009), and the individualism promoted in humanistic theory could also lead to self-centredness (Lahey, 2009). This theory has been accused of being naive and overly optimistic since humans are known to be more evil than humanistic theory cares to acknowledge (Lahey, 2009). Because of its subjective nature, selfishness, and naive understanding of the world, this theory loses credibility (Lahey, 2009). Rogers' use of unconditioned positive regard (Combs and Snygg, 1949), which uses an attitude of grace and accepting our failures, is also flawed for reasons mentioned above as well as Rogers' inability to use empirical evidence in research (Lahey, 2009). The holistic perspective of the theory does not help either as it allows for a great deal of variation and yet does not identify enough constant variables to be researched with true accuracy (Lahey, 2009). Psychologists also are concerned that such an extreme focus on the subjective experience of an individual does little to appreciate or explain the societal involvement in the development of personality (Lahey, 2009; Watt and Norman, 1981).

Psychodynamic Theories

Psychodynamic theories of personality are heavily influenced by the work of Sigmund Freud, (Sulloway, 1991) and emphasize the influence of the unconscious mind and childhood experiences on personality (Sulloway, 1991). The psychodynamic approach is heavily criticized for its unscientific analysis of human behaviour with many of the central concepts of Freud's theories being subjective thereby rendering it scientifically not testable (Sulloway, 1991). For instance, critics question whether it is possible to study such concepts as the unconscious mind or the tripartite personality scientifically (Bargh and Chartrand, 1999; Stroop, 1935); thus, it has been argued that, as psychodynamic theories cannot be investigated empirically, their perspective is unfalsifiable (Sulloway, 1991). Cognitive psychology has identified unconscious processes, however, such as automatic processing (Bargh and Chartrand, 1999; Stroop, 1935) and procedural memory (Tulving, 1972), whilst social psychology has demonstrated the importance of implicit processing (Greenwald and Banaji, 1995). This empirical evidence demonstrates the role of unconscious processes in human behaviour. According to Kline (1989), the psychodynamic theories comprise a series of hypotheses, some of which can be easily tested, some of which cannot, and some of which that have more supporting evidence than others. He suggests that, though the psychodynamic approach cannot be easily tested, that does not mean it hasn't got strong explanatory power (Kline, 1989).

Much of the supporting evidence for psychodynamic approaches, nonetheless, were from Freud's case studies; for example, Little Hans and Anna O. (Sulloway, 1991). The biggest bone of contention here was that the case studies were based on studying one person in detail (Sulloway, 1991), and according to Freud the persons involved were often middle aged women from Vienna who were his clients, thereby making generalization to the population of the whole world problematic (Sulloway, 1991). Also, the case study method is susceptible to researcher bias; re-examination of Freud's own clinical work suggests the possibility that he sometimes distorted his clients' case histories to reflect his theories (Sulloway, 1991).

Adherents to the humanistic theory criticize the psychodynamic theory for being too deterministic, almost divisive, leaving little or no room for the idea of individual free will (Sulloway, 1991).

Psychodynamic theory has been seen as sexist against women (Sulloway, 1991), as Freud believed that females were inferior to males, a result of his females' penis envy concept (Sulloway, 1991). He thought also of women having weaker superegos and being more prone to anxiety than men (Sulloway, 1991).

Trait Theories

Cattell (1965) disagreed with Eysenck's view of personality being understood by looking at only two or three dimensions of behaviour; he argued for the necessity to look at a much larger number of dimensions in order to get a wider picture of a person's personality (Cattell, 1965). Their modes of data collection are also a bone of contention, with Cattell using data from multiple sources: "Life data, such as scores from school grades, questionnaires designed to rate the individual and objective tests that tap into the individual's personality construct" (Cattell, 1965) whilst Eysenck collected his from hospitalized servicemen (Eysenck, 1952).

On twin studies, Loehlin, Willerman and Horn (1988) asserted that only 50 per cent of the variations of scores on personality dimensions were found to be due to traits, an indication that other factors including social factors were present (Loehlin et al., 1988).

The extent to which trait theories appear sound or convincing, it is asserted, is how well they are able to place in a particular class or group behaviours that can be observed, and whether application of standards or principles are not based on personal feelings or opinions but rather on actual evidence. Furthermore, even though theorists have carried out their investigations independently from each other, they have somehow all come up with similar traits results or outcome. (Aluja, Garcia and Garcia, 2004).

There have been criticisms also that traits do not accurately estimate or make known beforehand behaviours in every situation. This has created opposing suggestions that traits theories present convincing relationship between combinations of several similar behaviours. Also, whilst traits theories tell us how people act or conduct themselves, they do not make it clear to us by describing behaviour in more detail or revealing relevant facts or reasons to justify the conduct (Feist and Gregory, 2009).

Another peculiarity of the traits theory is that the individuals under study observe themselves or produce reports of themselves to be assessed; to produce such reports, the person must know himself or herself inside-out and be able to comprehend very well his or her own conduct and actions. This kind of data collection poses a real risk that the individual doing the observing might be biased and might introduce other inaccuracies (allpsych.com).

Chapter Four

Personality Disorder – The Concept

There is no sharp division between normal and abnormal personality functioning (Boyd, 2005); rather, personalities are viewed on a continuum from normal at one end to abnormal at the other (Boyd, 2005). Many of the same processes engaged in the development of "normal" personalities are also responsible for the development of a personality disorder (Boyd, 2005).

Personality disorders, as classified in the American Psychiatric Association's *Diagnostic and Statistical Manual of Mental Disorders, 4th Edition, Text Revision* (DSM-IV-TR) (APA, 2000), are long-standing, pervasive, maladaptive patterns of behaviour relating to others that are not caused by Axis I disorders (Boyd, 2005).

Definition

For decades, health professionals, including psychiatrists and psychologists, have had problems agreeing to a definition of "personality disorder" and have even argued if the term is really of any use at all (Moran, 1999).

The World Health Organisation (WHO) and the American Psychiatric Association (APA) have each produced a definition. The International Classification of Mental and Behavioural Disorders (ICD-10) (WHO, 1992) defined personality disorder as "a severe disturbance in the characterological condition and behavioural tendencies of the individual, usually involving several areas of the personality, and nearly always associated with considerable personal and social disruption".

According to the DSM-IV-TR (APA, 2000), a personality disorder is an "enduring pattern of inner experience and behaviour that deviates markedly from the expectations of the individual's culture, is pervasive and inflexible, has an onset in adolescence or early adulthood, is stable over time, and leads to distress or impairment" (APA, 2000). Each human being has a personality made up of his or her definition of self, skills used to relate to others, and a defense structure (APA, 2000).

Classification

Personality disorders are classified on Axis II of the DSM-IV-TR multiaxial system for diagnoses (APA, 2000), separate from the other mental disorders, which are classified under Axis I (APA, 2000). Separate classification under Axis II was intended to focus attention on manifestations of behaviour patterns (APA, 2000) that might be overlooked in the light of the more pronounced disorders of Axis I (APA, 2000); it does not imply differences in pathogenesis or treatment interventions (APA, 2000). Frequently, an Axis II diagnosis coexists (APA, 2000) with an Axis I diagnosis (APA, 2000), in which case the Axis II diagnosis may serve as the background through which the person experiences the other diagnosis (APA, 2000). For example, a person who has a dependent personality disorder might also have symptoms of generalized anxiety disorder when faced with demands to function autonomously (APA, 2000).

Given the above facts, and without going into a full-blown review on the epidemiology of personality disorders, which would be beyond the scope of this book, it suffices to briefly look at the epidemiology and description-classification.

Epidemiology and Description-Classification

The ICD-10 categorizes nine personality disorders whilst the DSM-IV categorizes ten, which are further subcategorized into three broad groups or clusters (Boyd, 2005), to which I shall adhere for the purposes of this book.

Cluster A: Individuals are described as odd or eccentric. They include people who are paranoid, schizoid, and schizotypal (Boyd, 2005). These people all have difficulty relating to others, isolate themselves, and are unable to socialize comfortably (Boyd, 2005).

Cluster B: Individuals have components of dramatic behaviours and are in the four diagnostic categories of antisocial, borderline, histrionic, and narcissistic (Boyd, 2005). Each personality disorder has unique features, each sharing a dramatic quality in the way the individual lives his or her life (Boyd, 2005).

Cluster C: Individuals are anxious or fearful and may have avoidant personality disorder, dependent personality disorder, and obsessive-compulsive disorder (Boyd, 2005).

Prevalence of Personality Disorders		
Clusters		**Median Prevalence (%)**
A: Odd/Eccentric	Paranoid	1.1
	Schizoid	0.6
	Schizotypal	1.8
B: Dramatic	Histrionic	2.0
	Antisocial	1.2
	Borderline	1.1
	Narcissistic	0
C: Anxious/Fearful	Avoidant	1.2
	Dependent	2.2
	Passive-aggressive	2.1
	Obsessive-compulsive	4.3
Source: Adapted from Mattia and Zimmerman (2001) Most studies report low numbers of subjects or none meeting the criteria for narcissistic personality disorder.		

In the UK, the prevalence of personality disorders in the nonclinical population was not known throughout all the early 1990s (Moran, 1999);

however, the epidemiology of personality disorder in the community during the last ten years or so appears to have been addressed by way of various research of nonclinical populations which used validated structured psychiatric interviews that had been purposefully put together to investigate personality disorders (Moran, 1999).

Here in Ghana there is no evidence of any such study being carried out. This makes gauging screening and assessment for personality disorders problematic. The prison service of Ghana itself does not even have a forensic service let alone a mechanism for screening for disorders. Personality pathology, therefore, presents a major public concern, which the people of Ghana appear oblivious to and which calls for a major research in this area.

Chapter Five

Identification of What Disorder and Which Theory: Full Needs Assessment Including Risks

A major problem that is of concern to practitioners in both criminal justice systems and mental health facilities as well as workers in primary care and social services is the treatment and management of persons diagnosed with personality disorders (McMurran, 2008).

A comprehensive assessment of the problems uniquely presented by an individual and his or her family and life situation is imperative to the provision of nursing care. Various teams must deliberate and draw up their own assessment guidelines that could be used as a framework. It will not help for each practitioner to draw his or her own individualized framework; it must be a team approach. The framework I shall be using here is the one formulated with my help by the Community Psychiatric Nursing service of the East London National Health Service Foundation Trust (formerly known as East London and The City University Mental Health National Health Service Trust, which assesses a client's full needs including his or her mental state as well as risks posed.

The purpose of the process of assessment is to create the opportunity to establish the conditions for treatment (Livesley, 2003) by building credibility, forging positive expectations about the treatment regime (Livesley, 2003), establishing a working relationship, and preparing the individual for appropriate interventions (Livesley, 2003).

We cannot eliminate risk altogether, but we can reduce or minimize as well as manage it effectively if it has been clearly identified in the first place. Risk assessment and management are at the heart of mental health provision (Eales, 2009), thus making it imperative for all mental health practitioners to be able to comprehensively assess and respond to the individual's needs and identified risks (DH, 2006a; 2006b). This clientele has a strong tendency towards impulsive aggressive behaviour, suicidal ideation, and self-harm (National Institute For Health and Clinical Excellence (NICE), 2009) as well as emotional dysregulation, which increases emotional arousal and reduces coping capabilities, which leads to impulsive actions (Livesley, 2003).

Sensitive questioning should illicit the individual's reactions to key developmental events and changes as well as whether the individual had experienced any significant incident of trauma, deprivation, maltreatment, or attachment, as these problems are rife in all the various types of personality disorder populations (Cartwright, 2006). Was support available? Exploration of interpersonal relationships is likely to reveal evidence of highly intensive and unstable relationships (Cartwright, 2006) as well as impaired social functioning, especially if a comorbid condition is present (Cartwright, 2006).

Full-Needs Assessment

History – Profile of Tamzin

Tamzin was born in the nineteen sixties and is the last but one of eight siblings and the second oldest of four sons. He was a very handsome little boy loved by everyone. During his childhood, marital discord caused his parents to separate and eventually break up altogether. The children were split into two groups; the mother took care of the oldest four children whilst the four youngest stayed with their father. Tamzin was one of the four taken over by his father. His parents' marriage like many, could be described as tumultuous, and his father did not spare the rod, believing he was doing the right thing for his children.

Tamzin was a child who loved food; if it was edible, he would eat it, which gained him a certain nickname that meant, colloquially, "food bin". His gluttony was so insatiable that, whenever dinner was served, even before touching or tasting his, he would start crying and say that his meal was too small compared to the size of his other older siblings' meals. It is reported that, on several such occasions, his father offered his own meal to Tamzin when the child complained about his meal being too small, and when Tamzin could not finish eating all the food on his father's plate, his father gave him a "time out" to teach him not to cry for more food unless he had already eaten his and found that it was not enough. After several such episodes, Tamzin learned to not cry for more food until he had finished eating all his own meal first.

After a while, Tamzin was sent to live with his grandmother. He was known to be a handful, and the poor old grandmother may have had problems coping with him, because he was later moved to live with one of his uncles. There he was found to be argumentative and quarrelsome. He liked to fight. He had difficulty negotiating anything, and his response to any unwanted or unpleasant situation was always to fight. He resented authority, and it is reported that he felt he knew more than his teachers at school so he never paid attention to them and was always on "time out" (excluded from class lessons) at school. It is reported that there was an incident in which a group of pupils from the same class as Tamzin, including Tamzin himself, argued with their class teacher and were all sacked from school, never to return. As a result, he left elementary school without completing the number of years required, so he had no leaving school certificate to show for any education he had achieved.

From there he was sent to live with yet another uncle who, by all accounts, was a kind and helpful man, but like all heads of households, he left for work every day to make a living. As a result, Tamzin was left at the mercy of his uncle's allegedly cruel wife. The wife of the uncle allegedly was a greedy, self-centred individual who did not take kindly to any member of her husband's family getting too close to him, including his children from his previous marriage. She reportedly mistreated not only Tamzin, but all the children in her care including her step-daughters. The work duties of her husband, Tamzin's uncle, took him all over the world. While he was away, the wife had a field day, it was alleged, mistreating members of her husband's side of the family. When the uncle was posted abroad, Tamzin was asked to go and stay with yet another uncle, but this uncle declined to take Tamzin in, saying that he did not have the means to feed him. Tamzin was returned to his mother at long last.

While living with his mother, Tamzin was involved in sibling quarrels and rivalries. This led to Tamzin constantly getting into fights with one of his brothers. Not knowing the challenges he had gone or was going through, he was invited by his older sister to come to stay abroad, but by this time Tamzin had taken to drinking, and he was drinking heavily. He was always seen drunk – day and night. In one of his drunken modes, he said something to one of his brothers about him (Tamzin's) moving abroad to stay with one of their older sisters, and apparently, all hell let loose with a physical altercation that saw this brother in a jealousy-driven rage threaten to pour hot cooking oil on Tamzin. With the help of one of his other older sisters, Tamzin consequently left Ghana to go and live outside the country.

Migration to Live Outside Ghana

Tamzin was eventually invited to stay with one of his sisters living in Nigeria. Like his oldest sister, the sister who took Tamzin outside the country was oblivious of the challenges he had endured and so did the best she could by finding him a job and continuing to monitor him. Tamzin reportedly moved from job to job, getting into fights and ending up in police cells in most of the cases. The police in Nigeria were ignorant about the issues of mental health and illness and never considered a referral to mental health services; neither did they even contemplate undertaking an assessment of his mental status. It is fair to say that the police in question were not aware of his background and what he had gone through, and so they can be forgiven for thinking that Tamzin was an average, normal, rational individual. Also, knowledge of mental health issues was not commonplace in that country I understand, and therefore mental health challenges were not recognised and so could not be addressed.

The challenges in living in a different country proved too much for Tamzin, and after more than twenty years, Tamzin decided to return home for good. He had missed attending his father's funeral fifteen years previously and was not going to miss his mother's too, so he came to Ghana to help with the funeral, returned to Nigeria to work for a brief period, and finally returned to Ghana in 2008, pledging never to leave. So far, he has kept his pledge.

Examination of Tamzin's Mental State

The mental state examination is a component of the full needs assessment of an individual, and it augments other assessment components (Lakeland, 1995) like the individual's profile and history of the presenting problems. The examination provides cues as to what additional details of the assessment need to take place; for example, cognitive assessment or psychometric testing (Lakeland, 1995).

The mental state of an individual is dynamic whilst aspects of his or her history remain static. The history is a means of structuring data relating to aspects of the individual's mental functioning, which typically applies a specific format followed by all health practitioners (Lakeland, 1995). All observations and findings are recorded under certain specific headings.

Some of the data is obtained either informally or through the other components of the individual's history (Lakeland, 1995). Both verbal and nonverbal questioning are used in a mental state examination and must be documented accurately, ensuring where necessary that verbatim accounts of the individual's speech and thought content are included. The following are the general headings, which can be subdivided: general appearance and behaviour, psychomotor behaviour, mood and affect, speech, cognition, thought processes, level of consciousness. Accurate examination of mental state requires certain skills, knowledge, and experience, which are only possible through appropriate training and expertise through years of continuous practice.

Appearance and Behaviour

Tamzin looks his age, over fifty-five years. He appears friendly, but his demeanour is almost always hostile, impulsive, intolerant, and impatient. He is tall and a good size for his height, and he maintains rapport in a hostile manner. He dresses appropriately for his age and season and is clean, kempt, and well-groomed most of the time with no body odour. He tends to look preoccupied most of the time, always laughing at his own jokes, and he wonders why no one ever laughs with him. He does not appear to have a sense of humour; he always appears to be suspicious.

Psychomotor Behaviour

Tamzin's gait is always brisk even when he is indoors, as if he is running late for some appointment or the other. He tends to pick his nose a lot, or so I thought, but I now know that he sniffs tobacco and possibly glue, and so has to constantly clear his nostrils so he can breathe properly. He appears to stoop a little, but this could be because of his height; he is quite tall. I have always felt that he is hyperactive and seems agitated most of the time. I often wondered whether he was abusing substances. I know he is an alcoholic who has made us believe several times that he had given up drinking, but I know he continues to drink when no one is looking. In terms of coordination of movements, he can be clumsy at times, but that could be deliberate when he is wanting to be destructive and/or seek attention; otherwise he is agile. He appears to be accident prone by the stories he tells of the numerous accidents he has been involved in over the years, but I now suspect that some of these accidents could be self-inflicted and a symptom of physical morbidity owing to drug and alcohol use, violence, self-harm, and risk-taking behaviours (Dowson and Grounds, 1995) correlated to traits associated with the cluster B-antisocial personality disorders such as impulsivity and recklessness or, possibly to insurance scams deliberately orchestrated to swindle money from his employers.

Mood and Affect

I can only describe his affect as mixed or dynamic, sometimes being congruous and other times being incongruous within a range of lability. I can say he demonstrates all the following: he is evasive; suspicious; hostile; angry; sometimes playful; guarded; very negative; and overly familiar sometimes, which can be inappropriate when he is trying to be friendly and pleasant and funny. Sometimes I get the feeling he is looking sad or could be depressed, but because of his reluctance to admit to needing or wanting help, and too proud to admit vulnerability, he usually quickly becomes elated, however any experienced mental health practitioner can detect the underlining irritability and anger. He is quite a pessimistic individual who very rarely sees anything positive about most things and situations. He likes to be regarded as knowing everything and being knowledgeable, but most of the time the opposite is the case, as he demonstrates ignorance, lack of self-esteem, and the accompanying anxiety mode whilst portraying himself as confident, and sometimes too confident. He likes to be seen as a very good and very nice person that everyone takes to instantly and easily and who is loved by everyone. He is argumentative, always wanting to have the last word; hence, he does not suffer teachers gladly since they always have the last word and know more than he does. Tamzin does not take kindly to anyone who appears more knowledgeable than him, yet he does not like to acquire knowledge formally or otherwise, not even through general conversations as he does not listen to others' viewpoint. I feel he could be suffering from a bipolar affective disorder, though I am told by those who purport to know him better than I, that his quiet and sullen moments could be a sign that he is hungry.

Speech

His flow of speech is rapid and expansive. He speaks with a lot of zeal, wanting to show he knows more than everybody else. He is forgetful but denies this and would argue that everyone else is wrong and only he is always right. He is loud because that's how he can keep a grip on his audience, which is very intimidating. His speech is always pressured, and he can talk about the same situation repeatedly if not curtailed. One needs to be careful also how one curtails that monotony, as he usually takes offence and lashes out reprisals. He does not take kindly to being questioned; to him it is a sign of authority, someone telling him what to do, and no one tells him what to do, according to him. He likes to offer information and to be seen as informative, but he gives the wrong information all the time, as he declines acquisition of knowledge. He is a poor listener.

Cognition

Tamzin demonstrates a short attention span and poor concentration, often with preoccupation. His memory is very poor for the most recent events, but somewhat average for past events, although it is difficult to ascertain the truth, as he does fabricate stories a lot. He is a concrete thinker, unable to handle abstract thinking, and he has no insight whatsoever into his mental status. He would deny it if it was suggested to him that he is suffering with mental illness. Anyone who attempted to tell him he had mental illness would suffer reprisals for "insinuating" such a thing. This would be a dangerous thing to attempt. I am sure Tamzin recognizes he has certain problems, but he would project his shortcomings onto other people, and blame them. He admits to not being well educated and dropping out of school due to circumstances, but he denies not being knowledgeable. He thinks he knows more and is more knowledgeable than practically everyone he interacts with, especially teachers. He just does not like being taught anything; he hates acquiring knowledge. He likes to make his own rules, and he likes everyone else to go along with what he says. Woe unto anyone who "disobeys" him. I am reminded of a Shakespeare quote: "I am Sir Oracle, and when I ope my lips, let no dog bark" (The Merchant of Venice, I). Sometimes I can't help feeling he has the perception that he is mentally ill but is in denial. However, it is also possible that, without the appropriate psychiatric treatment over the years, his delusions of grandeur have polarized so that he believes himself omnipotent. He is well oriented in time, place, and person. He demonstrates impulsive judgement; for instance, he does not take time to think about anything before blurting out the answer or decision, thereby coming out with or jumping to wrong conclusions and making unrealistic decisions.

Thought Processes

Tamzin is coherent but illogical, and his comments may even be irrelevant to topics of discussion because he is not knowledgeable about the topic and reluctant to listen. He just feels he must be listened to and not be challenged with the evidence or facts. He is excitable, demonstrates flight of ideas, and poverty of thought but would not admit to them. In terms of tangentiality, he deviates from the topic of discussion but does not acknowledge he is doing so. He sometimes has thought block, but does not agree he has.

Compulsion

Tamzin has a compulsion to vandalize properties that do not belong to him. He will spoil, break, or vandalize the property of others and then offer to repair it, just so he can be deemed a "guardian angel" who is so good and will spot your faulty household possessions. He then offers to repair them for no formal fees, but would expect a large tip or an extraordinary thank you gesture. He is paranoid about almost everyone and anyone with whom he comes into contact, eavesdropping on their conversations and discussions. In terms of delusions of grandeur, Tamzin believes himself to be higher and mightier than all and sundry, and believes he must be accorded the relevant respect of everyone complying with his instructions. Even when the decision is not his to make, he will make it anyway and expect others to go along with it whether they like it or not, whether it is appropriate or not. For instance, he might make decisions about how someone should spend money and manage finances, advising on what repairs, structural or otherwise, and how what he recommends should be carried out on someone's own personal property without discussions with the owner about whether there is a budget in place for the repairs, or whether the work is, indeed, necessary. He has an air of importance about him even when he is asking someone for food and shelter and for loose change. He feels superior to everyone and more important even than those who provide for him. It is not clear whether he hallucinates, but he has been heard to ask if someone was calling him, and when he is told he has not been called, he has looked surprised and suspicious as if he does not believe the individual and is wondering what's going on, thinking someone is making fun of him or cajoling him. Some of his compulsive and impulsive vandalism and destruction of my own household property leaves me to wonder whether he responds to command hallucinations. He also demonstrates ideas of reference, misinterpreting situations as being directed toward him. He has been known to also misinterpret situations relating to other people too, reading something into their situations when there is nothing to infer, advising something is being directed towards them when it is not the case.

Risk Assessment

Risk assessment by mental health professionals has been criticized ethically (Department of Health, 2007) because of its potential harm (Department of Health, 2007) to clients without justifying its benefits or respect to the individuals. Nevertheless, risk assessment is also a core duty as well as function (Department of Health, 2007) of psychiatric services mandated by several clinical and legal frameworks (Department of Health, 2007), particularly in forensic psychiatry (Department of Health, 2007). For this reason, it can and should be considered in a similar fashion to other types of medical examinations and interventions (Roychowdhury and

Adshead 2014), which includes not only the statistical properties of the process itself, such as sensitivity and specificity (Roychowdhury and Adshead 2014), but also using accepted models of biomedical ethics for its analysis (Roychowdhury and Adshead 2014).

Risk assessment in Tamzin's case includes risk of suicide, self-harm, self-neglect, abuse, substance misuse, violence, and risk of absconding.

Risk of Suicide There is no evidence to suggest that Tamzin would wittingly commit or attempt to commit suicide; however, his late father had a history of at least one instance of contemplation. This happened when Tamzin was a toddler when his father, my step-father, was accidentally injured when an incompetent medical practitioner hit his sciatic nerve during an injection. (I do not remember if it was a doctor or a nurse who made that blunder.) This turned into a gaping wound that was excruciatingly painful. In those days, during the 1960s, there was no such thing as pain management, so he was left to wallow in his pain for several months as the pain got worse and worse. Eventually it all proved too much for him, and he felt he would be better gone from this earth because of the pain. I don't remember what plan he had, being very young myself at that time. All I remember is people from the community pouring into our home and talking about him wanting to take his life, but I can't remember hearing how he intended doing so.

Risk of Self-Harm There is no evidence to suggest Tamzin would ever self-harm, but the above discussion is a family history. Having said that also, I strongly suspect and believe that some or possibly all the accidents he has been involved in over the years and talks so much about could be self-inflicted for purposes of either extorting money from his employers or for seeking attention or both, or as mentioned previously, because of drug and alcohol use, violence, self-harm, and risk-taking behaviours (Dowson and Grounds, 1995) correlated to traits associated with the cluster B-antisocial personality disorders such as impulsivity and recklessness, a symptom of physical morbidity.

Self-Neglect Tamzin loves himself too much to neglect himself; he loves his food and drink, and likes to look good. His personal hygiene, too, is impeccable.

Abuse Tamzin himself has suffered abuse from childhood, having been sent from pillar to post because of circumstances he found himself in. His uncle's wife used to wake him up in the mornings, allegedly, by kicking him in the head. Allegedly she starved him of food and showered him with insults about the small amount of food that he eventually managed to eat. It is the alleged abuse from his uncle's wife as well as being disciplined by his own father that would appear to have affected his self-esteem and confidence. Prior to his aunt allegedly kick-waking him every morning, his father disciplined him by using the cane. This makes him an abuser himself since the evidence suggests that abused individuals turn out to be abusers themselves (Sher and Trull, 1994). I felt that Tamzin had abused me, his older step-sister by disrespecting me, vandalising my home, my car, throwing away my personal property, and even putting rat poison in my food at one point. He also put a rat poison in his son's food too, I suspected even before he put it in my food. He has been known to abuse family members, friends, and colleagues in many ways that would be tantamount to criminality. Here in Ghana, however, the police system is so behind time in these goings on it is pointless to report any of them; the police would rather take a bribe under the pretence that something will be done, but absolutely nothing ever happens, leaving the culprit free to go on a further crime spree.

Substance Misuse As I have mentioned previously, Tamzin is a chronic alcoholic; he has misused alcohol almost all his young adult to adult life to the point that to see him sober is a rarity if not a surprise. It is not surprising to see him inebriated first thing in the morning. He also sniffs powdered tobacco, but it's not clear whether this is laced with some illicit or illegal substances. I suspect he could be sniffing glue too.

Violence and Dangerousness Tamzin is very violent, which makes him a very dangerous person to be around. The biggest problem is that, in Ghana, dangerousness is not seen as a risk; indeed, it's not even acknowledged. Danger is business as usual. Risk assessment in terms of violence, aggression, and dangerousness is not part of the language or the lifestyle of or indeed recognised by the people of Ghana. Neither authorities nor residents even appreciate that someone who is violent can put children and the elderly at risk. The culture of Ghana with regards to risk assessment is so bizarre that family members who are either demonstrating or threatening violence against their partners are often forced back together, totally oblivious of the risks to the other partner who may have become fearful for their life at that stage, and thereby vulnerable. They do not appear to learn from past lessons and experiences; it's incredible. Any person who can use a hammer to split a wall in two so the building just hangs, despite it being habited by individuals, is not just dangerous in my opinion, but is violent and dangerous.

Risk of Absconding Tamzin has been known to disappear from wherever he is lodging for several months at a time without letting anyone know his whereabouts. Then suddenly one day he reappears with no explanation of where he has been or why he had disappeared.

Risk of Exploitation Tamzin is not likely to be exploited by anyone because he is very streetwise and cunning. On the contrary, he will exploit anyone regardless of his or her status if he needs tobacco to snort or alcohol to top up his cravings. He is capable of charging more than he purchased any item for, and giving people excuses for not submitting a receipt. One of the reasons he vandalizes properties is so he can turn around and make repairs. His plan is to purchase the materials necessary for the repairs and then inflate the costs and produce no receipt. Having said that, this practice of tradesmen inflating prices of goods and materials they purchase for their customers is commonplace here in Ghana because of the reluctance of proprietors to supply receipts for goods sold because they themselves want to evade paying taxes through the taxation system. Also, the mentality as I have noted myself, of some sellers and utility suppliers is that giving a receipt is risky as someone else can take or steal the money and blame it on the person who signed the receipt. If they don't give a receipt, if the money goes astray in their possession, they can always deny ever receiving any payments or money from a person. When one tries to explain that, if money has changed hands, there must be a receipt, they quickly decline taking the money and the person requesting the receipt is asked to come back another time, presumably, when the seller won't be around and someone else will be collecting the money. It's amazing how their minds work with regards to transactions.

Summary of Assessment Including Risks

In summary, the assessments record that Tamzin is a difficult elderly man who has experienced many challenges that were beyond his control, all brought about by his family circumstances, which saw his parents' marriage disintegrate leaving him to be tossed from one family member to another. In terms of his mental state, he appears to be mentally damaged; he is paranoid, suspicious, and manipulative, suffers from delusions of grandeur, and splits members of his family including his siblings. He goes from one family member to another under the pretence of uniting them, but in fact what he says about one to the other creates more tension and fuels animosity between them, widening the gap between them thereby splitting them instead. It appears to be in his own interest to keep the siblings and family members in conflict and separated so that he can continue to visit them individually. In so doing, he receives free boarding and lodging and some pocket money to fund his vices. It would not benefit him if everyone got on well together. He is very attention seeking and pompous not to mention very cantankerous too. Tamzin's environment when he was growing up was tumultuous. His family had challenges, and his father physically abused his children repeatedly, such abuse disguised as "discipline". Tamzin saw his maternal grandmother, to whom he was sent after the parents' split up, snorting powdered tobacco, which was fashionable in those days and therefore was and still is acceptable. And we now know that Tamzin is hooked on powdered tobacco and cannot sleep without it. His uncle with whom he stayed after leaving his grandmother, was also an alcoholic, and Tamzin is now a chronic alcoholic. Tamzin is violent and aggressive and has been known to have had physical altercations with the mother of his son, a behaviour that was not frowned on in those days but is no longer considered acceptable. He likes fights and is argumentative and very controlling. The wife of one of his uncles allegedly used to wake him up every morning with a kick to his head; the kicks were so hard that sometimes he would experience headaches for hours on end. He would be starved of food and be showered with insults because of the small amount of food that he eventually would come by. It appears the alleged insults from his uncle's wife as well as the disciplining from his father seem to have affected his self-esteem and confidence.

In terms of risks, Tamzin is a very violent man, dangerous, exploitative, and abusive. He also misuses substances such as alcohol and ground powdered tobacco, which he sniffs. He also possibly sniffs glue. He leads a nomadic lifestyle, probably because of his severe personality disorder, which makes it hard for him to settle down as well as to find work so he can make ends meet. This makes it necessary for him to move around constantly, looking for work. He appears to be a hypochondriac, which could also be a ploy to receive sympathy and attention.

Chapter Six

Determination of Tamzin's Disorder: Identifying the Responsible Theory or Theories

Ascertaining Prevalence of a Disorder: The Theories Debate

A research undertaken in 2008 applying the Hare Psychopathy Checklist Screening Version (PCL:SV) showed that 1.2 percent of the sample scored 13 or more out of 24, an indication of potential psychopathy, and these scores correlated significantly with violence, alcohol use, and lower intelligence (Neumann and Hare, 2008). In the UK, a diagnosis of dissocial personality disorder is grounds for detention under the Mental Health Act in a secure psychiatric unit if they have committed a serious offence.

Behavioural Theories

Although it is believed that genes supply many ways for various cells to present, it is the environment, however, that decides which of them manifest according to the behaviourists (Cheney and Pierce, 2008). They posit that interactions between the environment and DNA are pertinent in the development of personality (Cheney and Pierce, 2008) because it is this interaction that decides what part of the DNA code turns into the proteins that will become part of the individual (Cheney and Pierce, 2008); reportedly, while the genome provides different choices, it is in the end, the environment that decides what manifests, assert the behaviourists (Cheney and Pierce, 2008).

As I mentioned previously, Tamzin's environment while he was growing up appears to have been tumultuous and challenging. He witnessed all sorts of behaviours from his extended family members, some of which he emulated and has become dependent on. It is the abuse from being kicked in the head and the constant disciplining that seem to have affected his self-esteem and confidence, judging by the literature. In his younger days, teachers were known to use the cane a lot to discipline children, so it is a possibility that his contempt of teachers stems from his contempt for being punished by them. It could easily have been a reminder to him of what his father had done to him. It could be that this demotivated him from continuing his schooling at the middle school level; he is known to have stood up to teachers, and my guess is he was fighting for his freedom from the punishment that he found everywhere around him.

The environmental challenges Tamzin faced would seem to have contributed to his faulty personality in terms of how he analyses, and what rationale he apportions to situations and events around and involving him.

Biological Theories

The biological basis of personality is the theory that personality is influenced by the biology of the brain (Plomin, DeFries, et al., 1997; Damasio, Grabowski, et al., 1994). Biology, it is suggested, is instrumental in the development of personality.

The Involvement of Neurotransmitters: Dopamine and Serotonin Pathways

The biology-based personality theories are based on correlating personality traits (Plomin, DeFries, et al., 1997; Damasio, Grabowski, et al., 1994) with behavioural systems related to motivation, reward, and punishment. Dopamine is a monoamine neurotransmitter that has been found to promote exploratory behaviour (Terracciano, Antonio, et al., 2009). Dopaminergic pathways have been specifically correlated with the extraversion trait of the five-factor model of personality (Terracciano, Antonio, et al., (2009). "The monoamine oxidase (MAO) enzyme has a preferential affinity for dopamine, and is correlated with sensation seeking" according to Terracciano, Antonio, et al., (2009). Could the fluctuating levels of dopamine account for Tamzin's craving for alcohol and tobacco and even food? He loves his food. Or is it the other way around? Do the alcohol and tobacco cravings account for the fluctuating levels of the dopamine, dopamine being a neurotransmitter that promotes exploratory behaviour (Terracciano, Antonio, et al., 2009), with the MAO enzyme having a preferential affinity for dopamine, and correlated with the sensation seeking id? (Terracciano, Antonio, et al., 2009) - food, alcohol and tobacco-producing instant gratification.

Serotonin is a monoamine neurotransmitter that has been found to promote avoidance behaviour through inhibitory pathways (Terracciano, Antonio, et al., 2009); "specifically, serotonin has been associated with neuroticism, agreeableness, and conscientiousness" (traits defined by the five-factor model of personality) (Terracciano, Antonio, et al., 2009). Could the fluctuating serotonin level account for Tamzin's demotivation for education and acquisition of knowledge?

Today's view of the gene-personality relationship focuses primarily on the activation and expression of genes related to personality and forms part of what is referred to as behavioural genetics. Research on heritability suggests that there is a link between genetics and personality traits. "Ever since the Human Genome Project gave the light for a much more in- depth understanding of genetics (Gazzaniga and Heatherton, 2006) there has been a continuum of debates on the involvement of heritability, personality traits, and environmental vvs. genetic influence on personality" The human genome is reported to play a part in the development of personality. (Allport, 1937; Skinner, 1984b; Damasio, Grabowski, et al., 1994). Tamzin appears to have inherited the violent streak from his father; indeed, he and his siblings were recipients of his father's wrath sometimes. His father, however, was a teetotal; he did not drink alcohol or smoke cigarettes or any other substance that could be smoked or snorted, so Tamzin's habits had to come via his environment as discussed above.

The above biological discussion suggests that biology in terms of genetics and neurotransmitters has affected and or contributed to Tamzin's faulty personality just as the environmental position.

Humanist Theories

Humanist theories emphasize the importance of free will and individual experience in the development of personality; humanist theorists emphasize the concept of self-actualization, (Lahey, 2009; McLeod, 2007; Maslow, 1999), which is an innate need for personal growth that motivates behaviour (Lahey, 2009; McLeod, 2007; Maslow, 1999). The theories of Combs and Snygg (1949) focus on subjective experiences of individuals as opposed to forced, definitive factors that determine behaviour (Combs and Snygg, 1949). They posit that the individual is good in the first place. Since I do not remember what Tamzin was like during his childhood because of all the times he spent with Grandma and other members of our extended family, I do not have concrete proof that he was good to begin with. However, to be rational, I can say categorically that, as a child, he would have had no reason to be unpleasant or obnoxious, that something had to happen to him as a child to even activate a trait if he was thus predisposed to personality disorder. Therefore, it would stand to reason that his familial situation and being maltreated by those who were meant to care for him by way of support for his mother would account for his predicament now. Therefore, being unmotivated to go to school to learn, and attacking teachers was a demonstration of him rebelling against his lost childhood for want of a better way to grieve. Every child has an unconditional right to be happy and to be treated well by the adults around him or her; in my opinion, Tamzin was very unlucky in this area.

It would stand to reason that maltreatment has contributed to Tamzin's personality disposition, which is demonstrated by his problematic persona, low self-esteem, and diminished confidence.

Psychodynamic Theories

"Psychodynamic theories of personality are heavily influenced by the work of Sigmund Freud, and emphasize the influence of the unconscious mind and childhood experiences on personality. They include Sigmund Freud's psychosexual stage theory and three significant components: the id, ego, and super-ego". (Carver and Scheier, 2004)

Tamzin, as a child, most likely did indulge in the pleasure principle of id for immediate gratification as demonstrated by his love of food, which caused his dad to constantly reprimand him. If bonding and attachment (Ainsworth, 1991, 1973; Bowlby, 1969) theories are anything to go by, then Tamzin would have sensed the unhappiness right from the onset while he was still in utero. He would have been born grieving already for what was to come to him, which would have developed his id so strongly that the ego and superego could not "get a word in edgeways" to save the day because of the pain Tamzin would have been in.

This would account also for Tamzin's psychosexual development as purported by Sigmund Freud; Freud suggested that in human personality development, what develops is the way in which sexual energy accumulates and is discharged as we mature biologically. Freud stressed that the first five years of a child's life are crucial to the formation of adult personality, and that the id must be controlled to satisfy social demands, which sets up a conflict between frustrated wishes and social norms. Both the ego and superego develop to exercise this control and direct the need for gratification into socially acceptable channels; gratification centring in different areas of the body at different stages of growth make the conflict at each stage psychosexual. Snorting powdered tobacco provides instant gratification of the needs of the id (the pleasure principle) regardless of external environment. In terms of Freud's role of conflict, each of the psychosexual stages is associated with conflicts that must be resolved before the individual can successfully advance to the next stage. Tamzin, it would seem, could not successfully leave this stage to proceed on to the next, and one of the reasons given by Freud for such a delay in progress is that the developing child's – Tamzin's – needs at a certain stage may not have been adequately met, in which case there is "frustration" leading on to "overindulgence" and "fixation" (food, alcohol, and tobacco powder are Tamzin's weakest points). Freud continues to posit that, in the first stage of personality development, the oral stage (up to one year old), the libido is centred around the child's mouth. The baby gets much satisfaction from putting all sorts of things into its mouth to satisfy the libido, and thus, its id demands at this stage are oral or mouth oriented such as sucking, biting, and breastfeeding. This oral stimulation, according to Freud, could lead to an oral fixation later in life, engaging in such oral behaviours particularly when under stress. As an example, Tamzin loves to eat. He will eat anything at any time; he has never been known to say no to food. And he loves alcohol, too, which has turned him into a chronic alcoholic. According to Freud, there is no further development in the latent (hidden) stage of five or six years to puberty, the libido becoming dormant with sexual impulses repressed and sexual energy thereby sublimated towards schoolwork, hobbies, and friendships, and acquiring new knowledge. So why didn't Tamzin sublimate his sexual energy (McLeod, 2008) towards school work, hobbies, and knowledge acquisition (McLeod, 2008), but instead ended up demotivated and eventually dropped out of school? (McLeod, 2008). Is this a flaw in Freud's theory? Or is this a cultural variance?

To what extent are we moulded by our culture? Are we totally moulded or can we transcend cultural influences? If we can transcend, how difficult or easy is it? How easy or difficult is it to befriend someone from a different culture? If it is difficult to step out of our cultures to communicate as human beings then it would stand to reason that who we are is moulded or determined by our culture, and therefore Freud's psychosexual theory is flawed given our cultural variances, his own culture to say the least.

Trait Theories

The trait theory approach is one of the largest areas within personality psychology. According to this theory, personality is made up of certain broad traits. A trait is basically a relatively stable characteristic that causes an individual to behave in certain ways. Some of the best-known trait theories include Eysenck's three-dimension theory and the five-factor theory of personality. Given the fact we are biologically determined, a trait disposition is confirmed. If, however, we are not determined by our culture as discussed above, then it would stand to reason that our rising above those cultural influences may be nothing short of some other determinism by physiological needs e.g. genetic disposition.

All the above evidence together jointly confirms the existence of a disorder in Tamzin's personality.

Determining the Disorder (Group/Cluster) and the Culprit Theory or Theories

Tamzin can be described as falling into the first two categories, clusters A and B, because he has some features belonging to A (odd and eccentric) such as being paranoid and schizoid, and some to B (dramatic) such as being histrionic and narcissistic.

Tamzin is paranoid and suffers from delusions of grandeur, which reflects the cluster A category. At the same time, he is attention seeking, histrionic, narcissistic, self-centred, and full of himself, which reflects cluster B, though he appears to isolate himself during functions while being loud and the centre of stage, which is very bizarre. Even though he demonstrates some excitable and extrovert features, there appear underlining antisocial tendencies; he can be seen isolating himself even when in company during a social event.

Paranoia Tamzin is always eavesdropping on conversations. He will hang around certain people or certain locations if he thinks he is being talked about or discussed. He quickly falls out with anyone he suspects of discussing him in his absence, even without proof. His suspicions are usually wrong. He is distrustful, demonstrates difficulty adjusting to change, is sensitive about issues that are not that important. He is argumentative and demonstrates feelings of irreversible injury by others, often without a shred of evidence. He has difficulty relaxing, has a short and a bad temper. He has difficulty with problem solving; he solves problems by attacking, fighting, and often vandalising property. He is unwilling to forgive even minor wrongs. He never apologizes, and never admits to mistakes or ever being wrong. He lacks tender feelings towards others. He has jealous streaks, and he envies people who have more or are more knowledgeable than he is.

Schizotypal Tamzin demonstrates incorrect interpretation of external events and believes that all events refer to him. He is superstitious and demonstrates ideas of reference, lack of trust in others and inappropriate and incongruent affect. And he appears anxious sometimes in social situations.

Histrionic Tamzin constantly seeks attention. He has a self-centred attitude and demonstrates sexual seduction and flamboyance. He is attentive to his physical appearance, is dramatic, and has an impressionistic speech style. He shows lack of conviction in arguments because of vague logic. His emotional expression is shallow, and he craves immediate satisfaction. He complains often of physical illness, demonstrating somatization; he is possibly a hypochondriac.

Borderline Tamzin demonstrates impulsivity as he binges on food and alcohol and excessively spends money he hasn't got. He demonstrates negativity and anger and easily feels bored. He perceives all people as all good or all bad. He tends to have intense, stormy relationships.

Antisocial Tamzin can be irresponsible, and he lacks guilt. He has difficulty learning from mistakes. Any initial charm he displays evaporates into coldness. He is manipulative and blames others. He lacks empathy, is very arrogant, is irritable, and has been abusing alcohol and powdered tobacco for years.

Narcissistic Tamzin has a grandiose view of himself and thinks he is superior to everyone. He feels he knows more than everyone, even though he is a school dropout and is reluctant to learn any trade. He falsely poses as an expert in electrical installations and repairs and plumbing without any training or education in those two fields, only what he has witnessed trained workmen do during their work. He has no formal knowledge of the underpinning rationale behind the practicals. For example, he might pressure someone to allow him to service his or her Toyota SUV without knowing anything about cars as a mechanic, or having undergone training by the Toyota company. He does not have a driving licence and has never learned to drive formally or informally. He knows only what he sees other people do when they are in their driving seats; he has never owned a car. He has an insatiable need for admiration and compliments and is preoccupied with fantasies of success, brilliance, and being the best person for everything and anything.

In summary, people suffering from personality disorders can demonstrate a wide range of symptoms at varying degrees of psychiatric severity because the clusters-classifications are so diverse (Alcoholrehab.com); hence, Tamzin appears to fit clusters A and B as shown by the descriptions above suggesting their presence in the presentation of his disorder thereby confirming same. It would appear by the evidence submitted above that all five theories have a hand in Tamzin's personality development being faulty; whilst the environment acts as a catalyst by virtue of his displacement and maltreatment by various family members, in terms of behavioural theory, alcohol and tobacco misuse act as catalysts to activate the trait and humanistic theories, with the biological theory reflected by the genetic aggression and violence purported by his father towards him and his siblings in terms of punishment. Four of the theories all appear inter-related, as the catalysts for the environment on account of the behavioural theory, as well as applying to the trait and humanistic theories in terms of innate activation and vice versa. Even the action of the neurotransmitters can be construed as brought about by alcohol and tobacco as catalysts, meaning that all five theories are very involved, and are somehow integral. The id in the psychodynamic theory can go some way to explain some aspects of the theory in relation to Tamzin's personality, but the psychosexual stages don't exactly fit; why didn't Tamzin sublimate his sexual energy towards school work, hobbies, and knowledge acquisition according to Freud, but instead ended up demotivated and eventually dropping out of school (McLeod, 2008) leaving a flaw in Freud's psychosexual stages theory?

Final Confirmation of Tamzin's Disorders

The evidence available from the full needs assessment including Tamzin's risk assessments plus the analysis of the information from the determination of Tamzin's disorder – the culprit theories, the responsible theories, the debate, as highlighted previously, against the backdrop of the current literature on personality disorders along with my personal skills, experiences, knowledge, and expertise in mental health practice, conclusively confirm that Tamzin does have a severe personality disorder of the psychopathic and sociopathic types of Axis II coexisting with bi-polar affective disorder of Axis I of the Diagnostic And Statistical Manual of Mental Disorders (DSM-IV-TR) multi-axial system for diagnoses (APA, 2000).

Chapter Seven

Establishing What Went Wrong: The Facts

Family Dynamics

Tamzin had seven siblings; both parents worked full time. His parents experienced the usual couples' arguments, and his father sometimes lost his cool. With so many children, it was difficult making ends meet, which was the reason both parents worked full time, leaving very little time for raising and enjoying the children, and for the children to enjoy their parents. Children ideally should grow up in family environments that help them feel worthy and valued (Stoop and Masteller, 1997) and learn that their feelings and needs are important and can be expressed and noted (Stoop and Masteller, 1997). Children growing up in such supportive environments are likely to form healthy, open relationships in adulthood (Stoop and Masteller, 1997). Sometimes, however, families fail to provide for many of their children's emotional and physical needs, and in addition, the family communication pattern may severely limit the child's expression of feelings and needs (Stoop and Masteller, 1997). In situations like these, the children are likely to develop low self-esteem and feel that their needs are not important, or perhaps should not be taken seriously by others. As a result, the child may form unsatisfactory relationships as an adult (Stoop and Masteller, 1997).

Tamzin's father was short tempered, and he reprimanded Tamzin constantly for his gluttony and self-centredness, which did not help Tamzin at all. A family in which conflict, misbehaviour, and often child neglect on the part of one parent occurs continually and regularly can lead to other members accommodating such actions, and this creates a dysfunctional family (Stoop and Masteller, 1997). Children who grow up in such families come to believe and understand that their experience is the norm. Dysfunctional families are primarily a result of co-dependent adults (Stoop and Masteller, 1997) and may also be affected by an untreated mental illness (Stoop and Masteller, 1997). Tamzin's father has a history of contemplation, which could be evidence of untreated mental illness. With the benefit of my experience in mental health practice, and in hindsight, I can see that Tamzin's father may have been suffering from a reactive depression on account of the extreme pain he was experiencing without any pain management strategy. So, can he be entirely blamed, then, in this case? This would require another case study, which is beyond the scope of this book. Being repeatedly reprimanded by one or both parents can have a serious impact on the emotional well-being and development of a child (Stoop and Masteller, 1997). It can impact his or her self-image, response to other people, and ability to form healthy relationships as an adult (Stoop and Masteller, 1997). Children who witness family discord can develop a sense of insecurity and feel unsafe, leaving them to think that the methods they witness are the acceptable way of resolving the usual mundane problems in life. This may lead to them developing symptoms of posttraumatic stress disorder (Stoop and Masteller, 1997). The Ghanaian culture does allow child discipline, but does not offer a definition for the kind or duration of discipline that constitutes child maltreatment.

Displacement

Separation of a child from his or her parents and removal of a child from immediate family or the setting in which he or she has been initially raised is displacement; it is sometimes done for a variety of reasons (Alfredson, 2002). Tamzin was removed from his initial home and his parents and forced to stay with allegedly cruel family members in some instances. It is a well-known fact that children thrive better both developmentally and psychologically when they live in two-parent families as opposed to one-parent families (Alfredson, 2002). There is a critical period that is sensitive to attachment development, which can adversely affect the child's personality if interrupted (Bowlby, 1969), since it's a reciprocal interaction between parent and child that helps the child to distinguish between his or her parents and other people, and to develop emotional, social, and cognitive relationships with the parents (Bowlby, 1969). This sensitive period in Tamzin's life may have been interrupted by virtue of the fact that he was forced to move around, which resulted in prolonged separation from his parents as well as prolonged exposure to poor care, including child abuse. All of this contributed to the fact that his childhood needs were not met, thereby interrupting the critical period (Bowlby, 1969).

A study by the Eunice Kennedy Shriver National Institute of Child Health and Human Development (NICHD) to assess the long-term outcome of non-parental care giving revealed that the characteristics of the family and the nature and quality of the mother's relationship with the child was a significantly better predictor of children's outcome (Fitzgerald, Mann, Cabrera, and Wong, 2003), and that prolonged separation from parents has profound disruptive influence on children's development (Fitzgerald, Mann, Cabrera, and Wong, 2003). Such separation includes divorce and desertion by a parent. Tamzin was deserted by his parents, in my opinion. His prolonged exposure to poor care led to despair, apathy, and a deficit in social responsiveness (Fitzgerald, Mann, Cabrera, and Wong, 2003). His failure to develop a secure attachment with his parents led to problems in social responsiveness (Rutter, 1979).

Abuse

According to the Child Protection Act 1999-UK, there are four different types of child abuse that harm children: physical abuse, emotional abuse, sexual abuse, and neglect.

Abuse to children can manifest as a single incident or several separate incidents that take place over time. Under the Child Protection Act 1999, it does not matter how much a child is harmed; rather, it matters whether a child:

> ➢ has suffered harm, is suffering harm, or is at risk of suffering harm (CPA, 1999)
> ➢ does not have a parent able and willing to protect them from harm (CPA, 1999)

Harm is defined as "any detrimental effect of a significant nature on the child's physical, psychological or emotional wellbeing" (section 9 of the Child Protection Act 1999).

For harm to be significant, the detrimental effect on the child's well-being must be substantial or serious, more than transitory, and must be demonstrable in the child's presentation, functioning, or behaviour (section 9 of the Child Protection Act 1999).

Physical Abuse has occurred when a child has suffered, or is at risk of suffering, non-accidental physical trauma or injury and can constitute the following: hitting, burning, shaking, biting, throwing, and poisoning (Child Protection Act 1999).

Kicking Tamzin's head, allegedly, every morning to wake him up was a very cruel act perpetrated by his uncle's wife. This act encompassed physical as well as emotional abuse. Physical abuse does not always leave visible marks or injuries. It is not how bad the mark or injury is, but rather the act itself that causes injury or trauma to the child (Child Protection Act 1999), as demonstrated in Tamzin's case.

Emotional Abuse occurs when a child's social, emotional, cognitive, or intellectual development is impaired or threatened. It can include emotional deprivation due to persistent rejection, yelling, teasing/bullying, criticism, hostility, and exposure to domestic and family violence (Child Protection Act 1999).

Tamzin was emotionally deprived by rejection, name-calling, teasing, criticism, and hostility. Domestic and family discord is strongly associated with child abuse and neglect (Child Protection Act 1999). For children living in a household experiencing domestic discord, there is an increased risk that their basic childhood needs will not be met, including the need for care and protection by their parents (Child Protection Act 1999). Tamzin was emotionally abused by those around him – the very same adults who were meant and mandated by nature and society to care for him.

Sexual Abuse: In England, child sexual abuse involves forcing or enticing a child or young person to take part in sexual activities, not necessarily involving a high level of violence, whether or not the child is aware of what is happening. The activities may involve physical contact, including assault by penetration e.g. rape or oral sex or non-penetrative acts as masturbation, kissing, rubbing and touching outside of clothing as well as non-contact activities such as children looking at, or in the production of sexual images, watching sexual activities, encouraging children to behave in sexually inappropriate ways or grooming a child in preparation for abuse including through the internet. (Child Protection Act 1999). Thankfully Tamzin was never subjected to any sexual abuse in his entire life.

Neglect occurs when a child's basic necessities of life are not met and his or her health and development are affected (Child Protection Act 1999). Basic needs include: Food, healthcare, adequate clothing, housing, personal hygiene, hygienic living conditions, adequate supervision, and timely provision of medical treatment (Child Protection Act 1999).

The alleged showering of abuse upon him at mealtime by his uncle's wife, including yelling and cajoling, was an act of neglect that would affect his self-image.

Lack of Motivation for Such Endeavours as Education and Vocational Training

Apart from having been compelled to become a difficult person to deal with due to the circumstances in which Tamzin found himself, it was the presence of physical abuse in the guise of discipline at school that demotivated Tamzin and formed a barrier to his progress. This contributing factor to the abuse of children results from societal attitudes that allow the acceptance by society of excessive physical force under the guise of discipline and punishment of children, particularly in schools, perpetrated by teachers (Child Protection Act 1999). Reprimands by teachers would have reminded Tamzin of his father's reprimands.

Attitudes differ across societies, but the following are the circumstances that inadvertently can encourage abuse (Child Protection Act 1999):

> ➢ Accepting the use of violence and force
> ➢ Accepting physical punishment of children

> Accepting parental "ownership" of children and the right of adults to treat children as they see fit
> Inequality between men and women
> Limited community understanding about the impact of child abuse and neglect on the lives of children

Substance Misuse

People suffering from personality disorders can demonstrate a wide range of symptoms at varying degrees of psychiatric severity because the clusters-classifications are so diverse. Research organized to confirm or refute the correlation between individuals who abuse and misuse drugs and alcohol, and people who experience personality disorder, proved conclusively that there is a link between the two, with traits associated with most disorders presenting during their adolescent years (Neumann and Hare, 2008). There are often challenges in differentiating between typical adolescent conduct and the presenting common psychiatric symptoms of the disorder, as I have come to realize during my work and career.

It is the lack of expertise in mental health practice and the inactive mental health service provision in Ghana that is responsible for the family not knowing what was happening in Tamzin's life. Even if they knew, would they have taken up any help offered in a way of managing his mental state, given the stigma that's so rife and stifling the judgement of the people of the Republic of Ghana, preventing them to seek help? Probably not.

Migration Challenges

Many people believe that, when they travel away from home, they leave behind all childhood and family problems; however, many find that they experience similar problems, as well as similar feelings and relationship patterns, long after they have left the family environment ((Bhugra, 2000; Cochrane and Bal, 1987)

I am sure Tamzin would have given a sigh of relief when he left Ghana to live abroad in "greener pastures" in those days, but events that took place in his new location sent him to police cells several times, and this would have been a force to reckon with. I feel very emotional for him.

This is because when people emigrate from one nation or culture to another, they carry their knowledge and expressions of distress with them. On settling down in the new culture, their cultural identity is likely to change, and that encourages a degree of belonging; they also attempt to settle down by either assimilation or biculturalism (The British Council, 2004).

It is suggested that elevated rates of schizophrenia and other psychotic disorders could be a consequence of factors related to the process of migration (Bhugra et al., 2000). Social selection into an emigration group could favour those with a higher risk of developing schizophrenia and other psychotic disorders, or the stresses associated with emigration might increase risks (Bhugra et al., 2000). There is evidence to both support and refute these suggestions. Investigations of the rates of schizophrenia in Trinidad and Tobago (Bhugra et al., 2000) suggest that they are much lower than those for African-Caribbeans in Britain and, in fact, similar to those of the white population of Britain (Bhugra et al., 2000). This would suggest that the higher rates are either a consequence of factors related to the emigration process (Bhugra et al., 2000), or of the circumstances surrounding the life of the emigrant (Bhugra et al., 2000). If the higher rates were a consequence of emigration, we would expect other emigrant groups also to have higher rates (Cochrane and Bal, 1990). Evidence here is contradictory. Overall, the studies suggest that other emigrants to Britain, in particular South Asians, do not have similarly raised rates (Cochrane and Bal, 1990). But King et al. (1994), in a unique prospective study of all ethnic groups coming into contact with health and social services in a region within London, found that the incidence rate for first onset schizophrenia was higher in all ethnic minority groups compared with the white population. In addition, if the higher rates were a consequence of selection into an emigration group or the stresses associated with emigration, one would expect the rates for those born in Britain to begin to approximate those of the white population (King et al., 1994). However, the studies suggest that rates of schizophrenia and other psychotic disorders for African-Caribbeans born in Britain are even higher than for those who emigrated, suggesting that factors relating directly to the process of emigration may not be involved (Cochrane and Bal, 1990).

An investigation into the effects associated with emigration risk status on schizotypal personality traits in a community-based sample of sixty-two

Moroccan emigrants and forty-one Dutch non-emigrants who were classed by the presence or absence of a family history of psychopathology, found that, overall, Moroccan emigrants obtained higher schizotypal personality questionnaire scores than Dutch non-emigrants, indicating that, primarily, those emigrants who are both intrinsically vulnerable and chronically exposed to social adversity are at elevated risk for psychotic and other disorders (Stelt, Boubakri and Feltzer, 2013).

Tamzin was intrinsically vulnerable and chronically exposed to social adversity, given his family circumstances and history, and because he was already misusing substances, he was therefore at a higher risk for schizotypal personality and other disorders (Stelt, Boubakri and Feltzer, 2013).

There doesn't appear to be any such studies or statistics undertaken in Ghana, so I had to make do with the ones closest to the investigations of interest

Chapter Eight

Conclusion and Discussion

There are constant discussions and debates in the UK about people with personality disorders, their dangerousness and violence, and how to effectively manage them. However, provisions for their effective management are always limited to psychiatric hospitals and units, and designated forensic teams. Community mental health nurses have a raw deal dealing with individuals who have undiagnosed personality disorders, whether they are living with family members or on their own. Because they have not been formally diagnosed, it is difficult to apply care management for them without reprisals. Generic Community Psychiatric Nurses need special specific training to detect severe personality disorders in their patients and to apply the mental health regulations on site prior to referral to the appropriate services, especially if the person concerned is not subject to the Mental Health Act-UK and not sectionable. Though in the UK this situation can present the Community Psychiatric Nurses in the community with very serious challenges, it is nevertheless manageable. In Ghana, however, the situation is very dire as there is neither similar mental health rules and regulations as in the UK, nor are there laws that do not support the situation, as it is with all the other laws in the country. The Community Psychiatric Nursing service in Ghana, if it exists at all, is not as sophisticated and well organized as the one in Britain, and Ghanaian Community Psychiatric Nurses are not specially trained to work in the community with specialist risk assessment and management training as is the case in the UK, making it the most dangerous nursing job in Ghana, most especially as there are no appropriate, efficient, and functional designated emergency services or out-of-hours services at all.

This means that living with a person with a severe personality disorder in the community in Ghana is like signing one's death warrant unwittingly. This is very worrying because, although I have not undertaken a formal study to exclude persons with personality disorders living in the community, as a very experienced mental health practitioner with extensive knowledge, skills, and experiences in all walks of mental health nursing, including forensics, secure mental health units, and prisons, I have been discreetly screening people I come in contact with and I can confirm categorically that, here in Ghana, in my estimation, at least 50 to 60 per cent of the general population is made up of people who have a personality disorder of some sort. In terms of mental health, about 90 per cent of the population is experiencing a mental health discord of some sort – depression, anxiety, and stress being top of the list with personality disorder and substance misuse coexisting in some cases at some points. But officials and citizens are either oblivious or in denial of this fact about themselves. The subject of mental health is a taboo in Ghana; it's not acknowledged in any way, shape or form. It is as if it does not exist, and if it does, it does not relate to the people of Ghana. Yet, there is heavy drug and alcohol abuse in the country with escalating domestic violence and criminal acts.

Evidence suggests that certain personality disorders compel individuals to take drugs. It is not clear which comes first, the drug and alcohol misuse or the disorder. Perhaps it depends on the individual with the disorder. For instance, some persons with the disorder take non-prescribed medication to lessen the severity of their symptoms and possibly to halt their emotional distress. Tamzin has always explained his sniffing of tobacco as a way of clearing his head, saying it enables him to see clearly. What exactly is he clearing from his head? Is he clearing the pain of abuse, of what he was going through as a youth, in his shuffling from family member to family member? Likewise, too much drug taking is capable of changing the chemistry of the brain such that it precipitates an onset of a personality disorder (Neumann and Hare, 2008) In both cases it is imperative that both the substance misuse and the mental deficit are treated to achieve the desired outcome of recovery.

In terms of discipline in education during those days in Ghana in particular, when a child was being abused under the guise of discipline, people may not have considered it any of their business (Child Protection Act 1999) or may not have wished to become involved (Child Protection Act 1999) or possibly did not trust child protection agencies and so would not report their concerns (Child Protection Act 1999) or simply that they did not recognise it as abuse. It is only when members of the community report their concerns for a child that effective protection of children will occur, and even then, it has to occur in a timely way so as to avert concerns becoming more serious and a child being harmed (Child Protection Act 1999).

Data on the epidemiology of mental disorders in Ghana is so abysmal and outdated, making it impossible to compute the burden of these disorders (Read and Doku, 2012). In 1984, a research on epidemiology based on the population of Labardi, a small area in the capital, Accra, gave an estimate of prevalence of schizophrenia in Ghana to be 2/1000 (Sikanartey and Eaton, 1984). Today this figure may be considerably more and needs to be addressed by a further well-structured research.

Personality Disorders in the Public Domain in Ghana – The Dangers

The lack of knowledge of mental health challenges in the public domain, specifically, personality disorder, and in general, psychopathology, is a real threat to safety in the public place in Ghana in my professional opinion. There have been situations in which clearly there existed a risk that was not acknowledged because of the ignorance of mental health involvement in the events that took place. For example, there have been reports on TV and other media regarding couples in conflict. Often in these situations, one partner, usually the male, makes threats against the female. Rather than keeping him away from the female, especially where there are little children involved, the family would rather encourage the couple to be together even though the female partner truly fears her male mate. Oblivious to the real risks, the female is left wide open to the danger and reprisals that an assessment of risk would highlight, which might lead to the management of the situation and prevention of any harm. There must be an element of a disorder of personality for the threat to have manifested or be realized. Even for the threat to have been contemplated at all would indicate some dangerousness on the part of the individual making the threat, and if the individual happened to be a user of drugs and/or alcohol, then there existed a predisposition that manifested but because of the lack of formal knowledge in this subject area, risk is not recognized let alone anticipated. (Neumann and Hare, 2008).

Other examples involve people placed in positions of authority who force demands on subordinates and who make threats and carry out the threats when they do not get their own way. Many of these individuals are heads of departments of various organizations and companies as well as public offices. They may make demands that are tantamount to being unethical by all accounts, but still expect their demands to be carried out. Subordinates fear that the superior will become agitated, lose his usually short temper, and carry out threats if his orders aren't followed. I was once asked by a colleague – a head of a department – to undertake a full-scale research in my own specialty of mental health and psychology and simply give it to him to use as his own to be eligible for the position of dean when the vacancy came up. I declined outright as I felt he did not fully understand the issues involving plagiarism and originality. Aside from that also, it would seem unethical for me to run around gathering and collecting data to analyse, just to pass on to some stranger I never knew until my appointment at the university as a lecturer, especially as he would use the information to his own end. I couldn't fathom why anyone would even consider anything like that, let alone make such a request and expect no questions to be asked. However, my refusal sparked a very unpleasant feud between us, which led to him yelling at me at any opportune time or in any opportune situation. He would send people to my office after hours to run the ink out of my laser printer to the extent that all the ink ran out in a week or so. He further went as far as taking from me his subjects that I taught and giving them to someone else. That act actually relieved me of the tight teaching schedule that I had at the time, but he was under the impression it was some form of a punishment. He was known to inflict similar punishments on people when they failed to do as he instructed. He just could not accept that I could not legally undertake a research or survey, analyse the data, write it up and simply hand it over to someone to make it his own when he did not hold even an iota of knowledge of mental health or mental illness or nursing or medicine for that matter.

The strangest thing I observed was how he would scream and yell at someone for giving him a gift because he felt the gift was not fit for a "king" like him. He felt so superior to everyone he was in contact with that he did not think he should be listening to anyone, even the university administration. He ran the department as though it was a school because he felt too superior to oversee merely a department. He would break the rules with regards to policy, refusing to recognize the university policies because he considered himself too superior to take orders.

I was fully aware of his personality predisposition to a disorder and heard several reports and complaints from fellow lecturers, which added to my discreet assessment of him, which led me to believe he was suffering from a personality disorder of a psychopathic and sociopathic types of Axis II coexisting with and gravitating toward depression at one polar and anxiety and mania (elation) at the other polar. Despite all the complaints that he was difficult to deal and reason with as well as that he was pompous, grandiose, arrogant, narcissistic, and lacking intimacy, no one considered carrying out a risk assessment as to his suitability to head a department or his potential danger to the university population. He was volatile and demonstrated streaks of violence even in the way he spoke when he felt challenged by anyone because of his grandiose ideation. He was very retaliatory and vengeful even in minor cases or situations that anyone would be expected to overlook. Being in his office was like being in a war zone. This was common knowledge, yet those in authority did not see it fit to do anything about him, simply shrugging their shoulders and saying he was a difficult one to deal with.

Such situations are quite frightening if one does not know what to expect from one moment to another, yet the people in the public domain do not take action when such incidents happen except to pay a lip service.

Risk and Dangerousness – Knowing the Signs

Assessing Risk in the Public Domain and Why We Need to Be Wary

For this book, I shall limit the risk to aggression, violence, and dangerousness only, but there are other risk facets such as self-harm, suicide, and self-neglect to name a few. Risk assessment is imperative in good practice in mental health and must be continuous as a critical and integral component of all assessments, planning, and evaluation processes (Department of Health, 2007). Any access to children also needs to be assessed regardless of what relationship exists between the person and the child or children (National Patient Safety Agency [NPSA], 2009).

Risk of Harm to Others: Dangerousness, Violence, and Aggression

There are many reasons for an individual to become aggressive and/or violent and thereby be deemed dangerous. Research has tended to be undertaken on the mentally ill or prison inmates, which in my opinion and experience distorts the findings because there is more aggression and dangerousness in the public domain than in these two target groups (Gorman, Raines, and Sultan, 2002). A person may pose a risk on account of his or her extreme anger towards another person for all sorts of reasons, and so it's imperative to identify during the risk assessment not only the source of anger, aggression, and violence, but also the persons to whom the anger is directed, as it may be necessary to protect them. It is necessary to ensure the person of concern does not gain access to the other person or to any weapons or anything that can be used to assault or harm, mar, or maim the one towards whom the aggression is directed. In very exceptional and serious cases, it may be necessary to inform the person concerned in order that he or she can stay away from the dangerous or violent individual, especially if the anger is towards a member of family who lives at the same address as the individual.

There are theories around aggression and dangerousness such as abnormalities in our chromosomes, imbalances in our hormones, and fluctuating levels and secretions of dopamine and serotonin neurotransmitters in terms of biology and genes as well as the individual perceiving his or her world as some source of anxiety in terms of psychology, whilst from the point of view of social learning, the person had learnt the behaviour (Gorman, Raines, and Sultan, 2002).

Nowhere in mental health practice is risk identification and management more crucial than in the community and public domain where there is always easy access to third parties including children, and elements such as weapons, and dangerous household materials, thus making community mental health nursing one of the most difficult professions in terms of risk to practitioner and to clients and their families. Historically, community psychiatric nurses have been at highest risk of violence, aggression, and dangerousness from clients and even those clients who have not been diagnosed and are therefore not known to the psychiatric service and who are substance and alcohol users. Over 75 per cent of psychiatric nurses have been found to have been assaulted at least once in their career (Poster, 1996).

It is, therefore, absolutely imperative that community psychiatric nurses are appropriately trained in and equipped with risk identification and prevention (risk management) skills and knowledge and must be competent in their application on a daily basis. Application of the skills and knowledge of risk identification and prevention includes and must begin with certain observations, especially when a client is to be visited at home. These include observation of activities outside of the client's house for example, cleanliness outside indicating the client is out and about with a vested interest in his/her surroundings; then the dust bin outside is checked whether it is full or has been emptied; if emptied, then all is well but if not then there might be a problem. Observe whether windows are open or shut: if open, then hopefully all is well but if shut then we must anticipate some disturbing activity inside. Then the Curtains, whether they are drawn, also an indication to anticipate that all might not be well. Severely depressed clients tend to keep curtains closed keeping themselves in darkness, therefore close curtains indicate the person may be very severely depressed, necessitating hospital admission. Then, has the letterbox been emptied or is it full and spilling over indicating no activity inside the house or flat, and thereby problematic. Inside the client's home upon entering the address, again the Community Psychiatric Nurse checks to see if letters are lying on the floor behind the front door through the letter box and looks around to observe the ambiance of the room whether it's clean; whether chairs or settees are appropriately arranged or just scattered around. Does the patient look clean, kempt or unkempt? What is the kitchen like, any signs of cooking or any culinary activity taking place there; is it tidy? Does the client look nourished and hydrated or malnourished and dehydrated? A look in the bedroom should reveal whether the client sleeps in the bed or stays up all night, an indication of mania which together with the diagnosed depression should suggest bi-polar affective disorder. Has the bed been made or sheets changed recently? These observations should be taking place before, during and even after a discussion ensues with the client and in the case of a new client, before a rapport is established and a formal needs assessment including risks are commenced. Not all Community Psychiatric Nurses or social workers are aware of this basic but crucial evidence of the client's mental state and subsequent situation during the crisis period, an indication that an admission to a psychiatric hospital may become imminent.

There is also a need for the public and society at large to know the signs of imminent danger to themselves and their families from an individual posing a risk.

Is the Damage Beyond Repair? Is It Too Late for Tamzin?

The clinical management of persons with personality disorder is one of the most challenging and sometimes controversial areas in psychiatry for two reasons: the clients have multiple and diverse needs, and there is much debate around treatability (Davison, 2002). Despite the difficulties in managing patients with personality disorder, their problems are easier to deal with if they are properly assessed and their individual needs identified and addressed appropriately (Davison, 2002). This is feasible only in an inpatient environment in a hospital initially. The mental health service in Ghana does not operate such a service since it does not have specialist services such as forensics and secure units where Tamzin can be effectively managed, and admitting him amongst patients on a general psychiatric ward would suggest the service has lost "the plot".

One reason that a personality disorder may not be diagnosed is the misconception or denial that a mental disorder exists (Adshead, 2001), given that, for a diagnosis of personality disorder to be established, "the enduring pattern of inner experience and behaviour, i.e. the symptoms, must lead to clinically significant distress or impairment in social, occupational or other important areas of functioning" (Davison, 2002). Therefore, the affected individual must acknowledge his or her predicament and be motivated to seek help. Tamzin would never acknowledge that he was suffering from a mental disorder, and any attempt to convince him otherwise would only be met with reprisals. Even the extended family would have difficulty accepting this fact since the stigma of mental illness will present members of their elite family with social problems.

The ICD-10 defining a mental disorder refers to "the existence of a recognisable set of symptoms and behaviours in most cases associated with distress and interference with social function" (WHO, 1992: P. 5), such as cognition, affectivity, interpersonal relationship, and impulse control; thus, the term *mental disorder* being applicable to personality disorder is much the same as Axis I disorder like bipolar affective disorder (Nakao et al, 1992) since persons with this disorder may need help as a result of their distress because the symptoms appear to interfere with their everyday functioning (Nakao et al., 1992). It takes a professional who knows about personality disorder to know if Tamzin is suffering from the disorder, but since the mental health service in Ghana does not offer its staff this sort of specialist training, it would be a very tall order for any mental health practitioner in Ghana to attempt to execute a diagnosis. What skills, knowledge, and experiences would they gauge against their attempt? If and when Tamzin is eventually diagnosed, where will he be taken for the appropriate and required treatment? The mental health service in Ghana does not have answers to these basic questions.

The New Mental Health Act

Passing of the current Mental Health Act in 2012 by the Ghanaian parliament was a big move forward and a major initiative in addressing the mental health needs of the people, the previous major revision of the mental health law having taken place in the 1960s. However, it is suggested that the act poses six major challenges to the health and social services in Ghana; namely, organizational, human resources, social services, and legal and judicial, role of the commission for human rights, and administrative justice as well as information systems (Read and Doku, 2012).

It is also common knowledge that the morale and satisfaction of mental health professionals and practitioners appears to be very low, and their perception of the way they have been treated within the Ghana Health Service (GHS) over the years is a very dim one, which may have been the rationale behind the original version of the act, which proposed a standalone Mental Health Service separate from the Ghana Health Service (Read and Doku, 2012).

Specialism and Specialist Mental Health Services in Ghana

The mental health services in Ghana have, by and large, remained glued to their historical origins of a medical model (Forster, 1962).

Mental health specialism and specialist mental health services are absent in Ghana; for instance, services for forensics, child and adolescent psychiatry, learning difficulty, and addiction are all non-existent in the country. Forensic mental health services in which mental health interfaces with the justice system needs special attention. Without this, the full realization of the potential of the mental health act will be severely compromised. There is no forensic psychiatrist in the country currently to undertake this very important task; the challenge to meet the mental health needs of this client group remains insurmountable.

There is a lack of research also of the treatment of psychological disorders in Ghana, which presents a major gap in the existing research. This, combined with the lack of detailed studies concerned with the interface between primary and secondary care, makes it very difficult to understand fully the processes which underlie the problems of access to specialist psychiatric care that have been identified in this client group. In addition to an inability to address important institutionalized cultural issues, there are also gaps in the training and continuing professional development of practitioners. Scanty allocation of funds and resources are not only inadequate and inappropriate, but are considered unacceptable to persons with mental illness. The Ghana health service has a duty to provide and support high-quality mental healthcare in this rapidly changing environment that meets the needs of the people in the twenty-first century, and provide more services and care outside acute hospitals, in the community and primary care settings.

The onus, it appears, is on psychiatric epidemiologists to prove the burden of mental disorder in Ghana and to demonstrate that the figures accurately reflect underlying patterns of the disease, and that there is a need for further carefully designed studies, particularly ones which are community rather than hospital based. As evidence, approximately 240,000 persons were estimated to be suffering from severe mental disorders whilst 2,400,000 were deemed to be suffering from some other forms of mental disorder (WHO, 2011).

Continuous Professional Development of Nurses in Ghana

The day-to-day activities that nurses perform are influenced and guided by various policies, legislation, codes of professional practice, government rules and regulations, as well as surveys and research, meaning nurses must have a working knowledge of relevant legislation and its application to their roles so as to be able to fulfil them effectively.

Ghanaian nurses, especially the recently graduated nurses, don't appear to have any working knowledge about the Nurses and Midwives' Council code of practice or the legislation or policies relating to their profession and don't seem to be interested in knowing either.

Nurses have a duty to meet the challenges relating to changes in demography, disease patterns and behaviour, lifestyle, public expectations, and information technology. They gain their understanding of their patients' experience primarily through direct care and from the literature; therefore, in order to provide efficient, humane, and ethical care, nurses must know why their patients behave the way they do and about the personal and structural factors that influence the way they perceive health, illness, and health services. They must know what factors facilitate or hinder their patients from adopting healthy living and lifestyles. These will be possible only in the face of a range of legislation, policies, and benchmarks that influence the ways in which mental health and social care are delivered, as well as motivation and a vested interest on the part of the nurses.

Treatability of Personality Disorder

By virtue of the association with mental illness, eating and drinking habits, smoking, accidents, and sexual behaviour, personality disorder is a public health concern. Individuals with this disorder, especially those who present with the antisocial and borderline cluster like Tamzin, have higher rates of suicide and accidental death than the general population, (Dowson and Grounds, 1995) with some of the traits associated with the cluster B-antisocial personality disorders such as impulsivity and recklessness contributing to high rates of physical morbidity owing to drug and alcohol use, violence, self-harm, and risk-taking behaviours (Dowson and Grounds, 1995). Tamzin demonstrates all the above.

The debate around treatability becomes polarized into treatability versus untreatability (Dowson and Grounds, 1995) with some asserting that the disorder is untreatable and so services don't have much to offer, which disguises a moral debate about responsibility for the client's predicament and about who deserves to be treated (Dowson and Grounds, 1995). The key features of effective management strategy would be based on the needs identified during the assessment as previously shown and would include services tailored to the individual's needs: prioritized, realistic, and explicit goals that are clearly formulated; long-term plans; consistent approach; tolerance and multi-disciplinary approach, the most important of all being, having explicit and realistic goals during treatment. There is also a need to have a shared view of expectations to prevent clients from feeling they are being set up to fail (Dowson and Grounds, 1995).

Even though more rigorous research is needed, there is sufficient evidence suggesting the viability of interventions such as pharmacological treatment and psychological interventions such as dialectical behaviour therapy (DBT) (Linehan et al, 1991; Palmer, 2001), which are reported to target problems of affect regulation and deficits in interpersonal skills and to improve social and global functioning (Linehan et al., 1991 and 1994).

Cognitive behaviour therapy (CBT) may be useful in targeting some symptoms and behaviours as applied in wider general psychiatric practice. Not much research has been undertaken to ascertain specifically its use in individuals with personality disorder but has been commended to be useful in targeting the dysfunctional beliefs that lead to maladaptive behaviours (Enright, 1997).

Cognitive analytic therapy also shows promise in borderline personality disorder management but is said to need further evaluation (Ryle and Golynkina, 2000; Denman, 2001).

Dynamic insight-oriented psychotherapy and "good clinical care" or supportive psychotherapy can also be explored in persons with personality disorder though it is suggested not to be rigorously evaluated (Dowson and Grounds, 1995).

For a small proportion of highly motivated individuals with personality disorder, treatment in a therapeutic community can be very effective in reducing both psychopathology and service consumption (Dolan et al., 1996, 1997).

All the above-mentioned treatment options would work well for Tamzin if he were motivated to acknowledge his mental disorder and accept treatment.

The questions now are: Is it too late for Tamzin to be treated? Is he beyond help?

All the above would suggest there is hope for Tamzin, but the following problems exist:

- ❖ The mental health service in Ghana is deficient in all the areas of the treatment options mentioned above.
- ❖ Tamzin himself is in denial of his mental status and therefore may not comply with treatment, so how does one broach the subject of treatment with him?

There is therefore an urgent need for reorganization of the mental health service in Ghana, first, to establish specialism and specialist services that can be applied to Tamzin and individuals like him who find themselves in a similar predicament. Mental health nurses must be adequately and appropriately trained in these areas to be able to manage persons suffering from mental disorders. There is an urgent need for a ring-fenced budget to revamp the mental health service, looking at training, recruitment, and retention as well as continuous professional development and evidence-based practice.

Integral to this should be public education and health promotion in mental health and mental illness at local levels as opposed to national levels to ensure the public is well educated in the issues involving their mental and psychological well-being. There should be purpose-trained health promotion practitioners to drive forward public education and promotion of mental health specifically.

With all these recommendations in place, there should be no doubt about the viability and feasibility of Tamzin's journey to recovery.

Chapter Nine

Implications of this Case Study

For Policy, Practice, Education, and Research

Policy

1). Ghana health service has been promised funding for new mental health initiatives in the past, only to see the money diverted elsewhere, it has been alleged; therefore, funding for health and community mental health nursing must be part of mainstream funding. A realistic target could galvanize new partnerships, provide earmarked funding for all mental health services in the country including specialist services, and drive forward the introduction of data systems that one can begin to trust. Realistic planning, earmarked funding, and local ownership are fundamental prerequisites for a targeting policy. A carefully managed process would be required and may need to be piloted. Health and social care establishments would be required firstly to produce valid and reliable data on its rates of compulsory admission against agreed and nationally specified criteria for key variables such as drugs and alcohol and diagnosis, which would need to pass robust quality control checks (DOH, 2001b).

Then, to enhance local ownership and engagement, rather than impose a national target, each area could be asked to develop and agree upon a local target. These targets could be published as part of a national benchmarking exercise, and earmarked funding could be linked to the quality and credibility of the plan. This would need to fully involve patients and their carers and families (DOH 2001b). New ideas would be required for culturally relevant but evidence-based service styles, family engagement, and models of assertive outreach (DOH 2001b).

2) Socio-Economic Determinants

The prevalence of deprivation and the concentration of social problems further exacerbate the underlying determinants of physical and mental ill health in the people of Ghana, social exclusion being therefore both a determinant and a consequence of poor mental health.

The issue of poverty must be addressed, and where possible its effects redressed; it continues to dominate discussions about the experience of certain group of people, particularly the lower class, indigenes of the upper north and northern parts of the country and the remote villages, to a degree that suggests that it relates directly to issues of identity in these populations. Issues such as educational underachievement, unemployment, crime, drugs, homelessness, and powerlessness will have to be addressed in a fundamental and substantial way if any meaningful progress is to be made in meeting the mental health needs of the people.

A realistic target would also send a clear message to people suffering with mental disorder and their families and advocates that their needs are being taken seriously.

Practice

1) Flexibility and adaptability in service provision, as well as awareness of the different social classes, is necessary to achieve an equitable system and thus reduce disparity. Without an acknowledgement and understanding of the serious omissions and discrepancies within current service configurations in most local areas, which leave some of the people at a disadvantage, however, there is little or no chance of the standards becoming viable in terms of making the service accessible, appropriate, and acceptable to them (Gilroy, 1994). It is fundamental to this understanding and to the setting and monitoring of relevant standards and outcomes that data can be analysed in local information systems.

2) *Physicians and Primary Care Services*

Physicians should be in a good position to detect mental health problems opportunistically. They are ideally placed to be aware of their patients' employment status or work environment. If patients are in poor housing, physicians can be called upon to support housing applications and offer benefits advice as an extension of treatment. They can therefore address the socio-economic and psychological factors that contribute to the mental health problems of their patients. There is a compelling case for appropriate training of physicians in the detection of psychiatric disorders in the lower class and the uneducated groups, especially where assessments are likely to be compromised by cultural beliefs (King et al., 1994).

It is therefore relevant to assess the demographics of the providers, particularly with regard to age and cultural allegiance, as this may identify some of the problems that result in dissatisfaction with services at both primary and secondary levels.

Community mental health services presently in Ghana do not address the needs of those with mental illness even though the definition of disability as defined in the Persons with Disability Act – Ghana includes people with mental disorders, suggesting that mental disability is not being addressed within the disability framework of Ghana.

Education (Training)

1) Concerns relating to nurse education and training are identified regarding the implications for practices surrounding diagnosis across classification of illness, and the status and influence of psychological assessments within the field of mental health (Burnett et al., 1999; Rawaf and Bal, 1998). Current nursing literature suggests that nurses and nursing care are often inappropriate in terms of attitude and mode of service delivery and that nurses must make positive efforts to emancipate themselves from their own values and biases, and take a metaphorical step into their clients' cultural world (Dobson, 1991) whilst others confirm that a lack of understanding of care needs across cultures is heightened by differences in cultural values and health expectation (Gilbert 1995).

This has implications for the curriculum in that, while certain subject areas are allocated significantly more time, others may be omitted from the curriculum. This in turn contributes to omission of key learning, thereby preventing the delivery of socially and culturally sensitive care (Ouseley, 1997). There are no signs that the vital objective of equipping the profession to serve the twenty-first century multiracial society is being met in Ghana (Gilbert, 1995). It is imperative that nurses improve their understanding and awareness of the racial and cultural needs of people who use the mental health services and ensure that these are fully reflected when developing care plans, since Ghana is now a multi-racial and thereby a multi-cultural country, which means that the expression of symptoms can be at variance among clients of many cultures, and may reflect cultural patterns; for example, the content of delusions and hallucinations (Burnett et al., 1999; Rawaf and Bal, 1998.)

2) Public Education and Advocacy Service

There is a need for public education in mental health and illness and health promotion. Advocacy is also needed in other aspects of mental health ranging from general advice about services to more specific information and advice about medication, therapies, welfare, and other rights.

Research

1) There is a dearth of literature, highlighted by this case study on personality disorders and on mental health generally in Ghana, and this must be addressed so those in authority will be able to strategize and meet targets.

The review of the literature during this case study has highlighted that many basic questions concerning the relationship between ethnicity and mental health remain unanswered. There remains a question of whether the use of Western psychiatric instruments for the cross-cultural measurement of psychiatric disorder is valid and produces a genuine reflection of the differences between different ethnic groups (Gilbert, 1995; Bhugra et al., 2000), particularly in relation to the low detection and treatment rates for other psychiatric disorders such as anxiety, depression, and personality disorder (Gilbert, 1995; Bhugra et al., 2000). It is also possible that treatment-based statistics do not accurately reflect the experiences of the ethnic population from which those in treatment were drawn (Li et al., 1994; Mukhopadhyay, 2000; Bhugra et al., 2000). The literature on ethnicity and mental health suggests a need for better data in this area (Bhugra et al., 2000).

2) Also, from an aetiological perspective, there is a need to explore the factors associated with ethnicity that may explain any relationship between ethnicity and mental health, such as the various forms of social disadvantage that the people face; for example, difficulty accessing services, housing problems, educational underachievement, and culturally appropriate services (Bhugra et al., 2000). These can be explored adequately only within a sample that includes both the ill and not ill, so that the experiences of the two groups can be explored.

Mental health is a neglected area in healthcare in Ghana with few clinicians, specialists, and trained researchers in this field; research has been limited both in quantity and quality. The existing literature suggests several important areas for future research that would inform the development of targeted and effective interventions in mental healthcare in Ghana.

Epidemiological data is scarce and unreliable with no large-scale studies having been published. There are very few studies of clinical practice in mental health, and all of them were undertaken by researchers from developed countries overseas.

Chapter Ten

Recommendations and Future Works

For Policy, Practice, Education, and Research

1. Policy

- ❖ In 2008, Ghana had only ten psychiatrists compared with some 13,074 medical doctors to the population of 24, 252,438 (Ghana Health Service, Facts and Figures, 2009). This disparity calls for an urgent redress.
- ❖ The country profile of the Ghana Human Resource for Health does not reflect issues on mental health workforce (Ghana Health Workforce Observatory, 2011). There is therefore an urgent need for a human resource strategy that would address recruitment, retention, professional development, and challenges of the mental health workforce.
- ❖ A greater financial commitment from the health service towards consultation with mentally ill clients would be extremely useful. Discussions with clients, their families, and stakeholders would reveal their perspective on treatment. There is a high incidence of drug and alcohol use in Ghana presently.
- ❖ Information should be made available, through information centres or mental health consultants groups, of alternative services and where to access appropriate treatment.
- ❖ Planners need to act now to deliver mental health services appropriate to the needs of the people, and steer mental health services in the direction of treatment equality.

❖ There must be better communication, coordination, and collaboration with community organizations for care coordinating and care planning for patients leaving hospital and returning to the community; strategies are needed at all levels to target key groups who under use existing services.

❖ Also, new initiatives should be introduced that are directed at people who are most likely to be unwell but least likely to access services.

❖ When services are being developed, or reviewed, purchasers and providers should look at how different communities use psychiatric facilities.

❖ Primary care must meet their responsibilities by commissioning culturally appropriate and effective services that meet the specific needs of their local populations. They must also ensure that there is a balance between services for more common mental health problems and for those suffering from severe and enduring mental illness.

❖ Primary care must develop structures that will support and facilitate more effective liaison between the different professionals who are involved in delivering mental health services.

❖ It is imperative that there is consistent and robust monitoring and evaluation of primary care mental health services and that the process must involve patients and their carers to ensure that local standards are in line with the National Service standards.

❖ Early detection is another area in which innovative strategies are urgently needed. Given that young people are reluctant to engage with primary care services, it is essential that ways be found to either encourage their access to such services or provide services in alternative settings.

❖ Primary care must develop meaningful and equitable partnerships with non-governmental organizations, to bridge the considerable gap between the services provided and the needs of members of the communities served by the non-governmental organizations.

2. Practice

❖ To establish the validity of diagnostic categories across cultures, careful attention needs to be paid to the expression of individual symptoms and the relationship between the professional and the assumed notion of what constitutes distress and disorder.

❖ The Mental Health Act passed in Ghana has social implications as well as health implications; therefore, the financing of mental healthcare would not be the sole responsibility of the Ministry of Health. There is a compelling case for collaboration between the Ministries of Employment and Social Welfare, Finance and Economic Planning, and local government to ensure an effective implementation of the act (Akondo, 2011).

❖ The education sector has a key role to play and must develop strategies for young people that can improve their attainment and promote their mental health and well-being.

❖ It is essential that protocols be instituted to ensure that patients and their carers, or their nominated representatives are consulted automatically and involved in all aspects of their care. This consultation process should include all matters of policy development and service planning and development, as well as involvement in individual care planning. The needs of carers must also be considered and catered for.

3. Training

❖ Nurse training must recognize diversity. Not training staff to address the needs of a multi-racial society is an appalling indictment on the Ghana Health Service. Nurses must recognize cultural differences so they can give the best care.

❖ There is a compelling case for appropriate training of physicians in the detection of psychiatric disorders in their clients, especially where assessments are likely to be compromised by cultural beliefs.

❖ It is very strongly recommended that a comprehensive inter-agency training programme be developed to train primary care group staff, hospital doctors, nurses, social workers, and other care and support staff and the police on the following (Rawaf and Bahl, 1998; Modood et al., 1997; Gilbert, 1994):
- Mental health and cultural competence programmes
- Mental health promotion and education
- Diversity management
- Understanding the needs of migrants and refugees

- Equality and anti-discriminatory practice
- Good practice guidelines
- Risk assessment, management, and reduction

4. Research

❖ Services should therefore employ interdisciplinary research methods that integrate anthropological and epidemiological frameworks (Weiss et al., 1995).

❖ More detailed analyses of patient samples that consider differences in economic circumstances are vital. This would help elucidate whether particular cultures have a protective effect, or whether ethnicity combined with privation, isolation, and discrimination put people at greater risk.

❖ There is also a need to commission research with study designs and sample sizes that will convincingly address the problems of confounding by age, gender, and socio-economic factors, and case definition.

❖ Researchers need to demonstrate sensitivity to questions relevant to disorders of the patients and the anxiety of their carers as well as to those who must deliver evidence-grounded healthcare given the ambiguity of patients about accepting their illness.

❖ We need qualitative methods too, and these can be nested in larger-scale quantitative studies that examine the role of cultural factors in access to care, pathways through service, and the duration of untreated psychosis.

❖ There is a need for larger samples studies that allow the findings to be generalized.

Priorities for mental health research in Ghana: according to Read & Doku, 2012

❖ Population-based epidemiological studies of mental disorders – including attention to shrines and churches (Read and Doku, 2012)

❖ Research on mental disorders, specifically psychosis, substance use, depression, somatisation, and self-harm including risk factors, clinical picture, course, and outcome (Read and Doku, 2012)

- ❖ Outcome studies of interventions within psychiatric services, primary care and other service providers; for example, non-governmental organizations (NGOs) (Read and Doku, 2012)
- ❖ Experiences of people with mental illness and their family members, including the psychosocial and financial impact, help-seeking, and treatment experiences (Read and Doku, 2012)
- ❖ The practices of traditional and religious healers and potential for collaboration (Read and Doku, 2012)

References

Adshead, G. (2001), "Murmurs of discontent: Treatment and treatability of personality disorder". *Advances in Psychiatric Treatment, 7*, 407–415.

Adomakoh, C. C. (1972), "Mental hospital patients: A Castle Road profile". *Ghana Medical Journal.* **2**, 65–71.

Adorno, T. W., Frenkel-Brunswik, E., Levinson, D. J., and Sanford, R. N. (1950) "The authoritarian personality". *New York: Harper and Row.*

Ainsworth, M. D. S. (1991) "Attachments and other affectional bonds across the life cycle. In C. M. Parkes, J. Stevenson-Hinde, and P. Marris (Eds.), Attachment across the life cycle" London: Routledge. 33–51.

Ainsworth, M. D. S. (1973) "The development of infant-mother attachment. In B. Cardwell and H. Ricciuti (Eds.), Review of child development research Chicago". University of Chicago Press. Vol. 3, 1–94

Akondo N. (2011) "Rethinking Mental Health Bill: Some Thoughts on Financial Implications". http://opinion.myjoyonline.com/pages/feature/201203/82400.php (accessed 15 November 2012).

Alfredson, Lisa, (2002) "Child Soldiers, Displacement and Human Security". *Disarmament Forum 4, l 7–27*

Allport, G. W. (1937) "Personality: a psychological interpretation, in W. J. Livesley (ed) Practical Management of Personality Disorder". New York: Guilford Press

Allport, G. W. (1937) Personality: "A psychological interpretation". H. Holt and. Company: New York

Aluja, A., García, Ó. and García, L. F. (2004) "Replicability of the three, four and five Zuckerman's personality super-factors: Exploratory and confirmatory factor analysis of the EPQ-RS, ZKPQ and NEO-PI-R". *Personality and Individual Differences* 36 (5): 1093–1108. Doi: 10.1016/S0191-8869(03)00203-4.

American Psychiatric Association (APA) (2000) "*Diagnostic and Statistical Manual of Mental Disorders. 4th edn. Text revision (DSM-IV-TR)*". Washington, DC

Bandura, A. (1977). "Social learning theory". Englewood Cliffs, NJ: Prentice Hall

Bargh, J. A., and Chartrand, T. L. (1999). "The unbearable automaticity of being". American psychologist, 54(7), 462.

Boulding, K. E. (1984) "B. F. Skinner: A dissident view". *Behavioural and Brain Sciences,* 7, 48–484

Bowlby J. (1969). "Attachment. Attachment and loss: Vol. 1. Loss". New York: Basic Books.

Boyd, M. A. (2005) "Psychiatric Nursing Contemporary Practice". Lippincott Williams and Wilkins: New York.

Bhugra, D. (2000) "Migration and schizophrenia". *Acta Psychiatrica Scandinavica,* Volume 102, Issue 407 68–73

Bhugra, D. and Bhui, K. (2001) "Cross-Cultural Psychiatry: A Practical Guide". London: Arnold.

Bhugra, D., Hilwig, M., Hussein, B., Marceau, H., Neehall, J., Leff, J., Mallett, R., and Der, G. (1996) "First Contact Incidence Rates of Schizophrenia in Trinidad and One-Year Follow-Up". *British Journal of Psychiatry,* Vol 169; pp 587–592

Bhugra, D., Leff, J., Mallet, R., et al (1997) "Inception Rates and One Year Outcome of Schizophrenia in West London". *Psychological Medicine*, 27, 791–798

Bhugra, D. and Bhui, K. (1998) "Transcultural Psychiatry: Do Problems Persist in the Second Generation"? *Hospital Medicine*, 59, 126–129

Bhugra, D., Hilwig, M., Mallett, R., Corridan, B., Leff, J., Neehall, J., Rudge, S. (2000) "Factors in the onset of Schizophrenia: A Comparison between London and Trinidad Samples". Acta Psychiatrica Scandinavica Vol. 101, Issue 2, page 135.

Carver, C., and Scheier, M. (2004). "Perspectives on Personality (5th Ed.)". Boston: Pearson.

Castillo, H. (2009) "The Person with a personality disorder, in I. Norman and I. Ryrie (eds.) The Art and Science of Mental Health Nursing: A Textbook of Principles and Practice, 2nd edn." Maidenhead: McGraw-Hill

Cattell, R. B. (1965). "The scientific analysis of personality". Baltimore: Penguin Books.

Cheney, W. David Pierce, Carl D. (2008). "Behaviour analysis and learning (4th Ed.)". New York, NY: *Psychology Press*. ISBN 9780805862607.

Cochrane R. and Bal SS. (1987) "Migration and schizophrenia: an examination of five hypotheses". *British Medical Bulletin*, Vol. 69 Social Psychiatry; 22: 180–91 5.

Cochrane, R. & Bal, S.S. (1990) "Mental Hospital Admission Rates of Immigrants to England: A Comparison of 1971 and 1981". Social Psychiatry and Psychiatric Epidemiology, 24, 2-12.

Combs, Arthur W., and Snygg, Donald. (1949) "A New Frame of Reference for Psychology". New York, Harper and Brothers. *Article on Snygg and Combs' Phenomenological Field Theory*

Cordall, J. (2009) "Risk assessment and management, in P. Woods and A. M. Kettles (eds) Risk Assessment and Management in Mental Health Nursing". Oxford: Blackwell Livingstone

Corr, P.J. (2007). "Personality and Psychology. Hans Eysenck's Unifying Themes". Hans Eysenck Memorial Lecture, Psychology, 11, 7, 666–669

Dahlbom, B. (1984) "B. F. Skinner, selection, and self-control". *Behavioural and Brain Sciences, 7, 484–486.*

Davey, G. (2008) "Psychopathology: Research, Assessment and Treatment in Clinical Psychology". Leicester: British Psychological Society and Blackwall Publishing

David Stoop and James Masteller (1997). "Forgiving Our Parents, Forgiving Ourselves: Healing Adult Children of Dysfunctional Families". Regal. ISBN 978-0830734238

Davison, S. E. (2002) "Principles of Managing Patients with Personality Disorder". Advances in Psychiatric Treatment. *British Journal of Psychiatry* London

Denman, C. (2001) "Cognitive–analytic therapy". *Advances in Psychiatric Treatment, 7, 342–256.*

Department of Health (DH) (2007) "Best practice in managing risk: Principles and evidence for best practice in the assessment and management of risk to self and others in mental health services". London: Department of Health.

DeYoung, Colin G. (2010). *"Personality Neuroscience and the Biology of Traits". Social and Personality Psychology Compass* 4 (12): 1165–1180. Doi: 10.1111/j.1751-9004.2010. 00327. x. ISSN 1751-9004

D.O.H (2001b) "Shifting the balance of power within the National Health Service: securing delivery" London, Department of Health.

Dolan, B. M., Warren, F. M., and Menzies, D., et al (1996) "Cost-offset following specialist treatment of severe personality disorders". *Psychiatric Bulletin*, 20, 413–417.

Dowson, J. H. and Grounds, A. T. (Eds) (1995) "Personality disorders, recognition and clinical management". Cambridge: Cambridge University Press.

Enright, S. J. (1997) "Cognitive behaviour therapy – clinical applications". *British Medical Journal,* 314, 1811–1816.

Eysenck, H. J. (1952) "The scientific study of personality". Routledge and K. Paul,

Eysenck, H. J. (1966) "Personality and experimental psychology". *Bulletin of the British Psychological Society.*

Eysenck, H. J. (1967) "The biological basis of personality". Transaction publishers. Vol. 689.

Eysenck, H. J. (1982) "Personality, genetics, and behaviour": Selected papers.

Feist, Jess Feist, Gregory J. (2009) "Theories of personality (7th Ed.)" Boston: McGraw Hill Higher Education. ISBN 978-0-07-338270-8.

Fitzgerald, H., Mann, T., Cabrera, N., and Wong, M. (2003) "Diversity in caregiving contexts in R. Lerner, A. Easterbrooks, and J. Mistry (Eds.)". Mahwah, NJ: Lawrence Erlbaum. *Handbook of psychology, Vol 6: Developmental psychology*. 135-167.

Forster E. B. (1962) "A historical survey of psychiatric practice in Ghana". *Ghana Medical Journal*.1:25–29.

Forster E. B. (1971) "Forensic attitudes in the delivery of mental healthcare in Ghana". *Ghana Medical Journal*. 1971; 10(1):52–55.

Freud, S. (1905) "Three essays on the theory of sexuality". SE, 7.

Freud, S. (1920*)* "Beyond the pleasure principle". SE, 18: 1–64.

Freud, S. (1923) "The ego and the id". SE, 19: 1–66.

Ghana Health Service. (2009) "The Health Sector in Ghana-Facts and Figures". The Ghana Health Service Annual Report and Ghana Health Service Annual Statistical Report.

Ghana Health Workforce Observatory (2011) "Ghana Human Resources for Health Profile". Ghana Statistical Service. (2010) "Population and Housing Census-Summary report of final results".

Greenwald, A. G., and Banaji, M. R. (1995) "Implicit social cognition: attitudes, self-esteem, and stereotypes". *Psychological review*, 102(1), 4.

Gross, R. (2010) "Psychology: The Science of Mind and Behaviour, 6th edn." London: Hodder

Hyman, H. H., and Sheatsley, P. (1956) "Attitudes Toward Desegregation". *Scientific American,* 195:35–39.

Jarrett, C. (2006) "Understanding Personality Disorder, The Psychologist" 19(7): 402-4

Kahn, Michael (2002*)* "Basic Freud: psychoanalytic thought for the twenty first century" (1. paperback Ed.). New York: Basic Books. ISBN 9780465037162.

Kline, P. (1989). "Objective tests of Freud's theories". Psychology Survey, 7, 127–45.

Lahey, B. B. (2009) "Psychology: An introduction (10th Ed.)" New York: McGraw-Hill.

Linehan, M. M., Tutek, D. A., Heard, H. L, et al (1994) "Interpersonal outcome of cognitive behavioural treatment of chronically suicidal borderline patients". *American Journal of Psychiatry,* 151, 1771–1776.

Linehan, M., Armstrong, H., Suarez, A., et al (1991) "Cognitive behavioural treatment of chronically Para suicidal borderline patients". Archives of General Psychiatry, 48, 1060–1064.

Loehlin, J. C., Willerman, L., and Horn, J. M. (1988). "Human behaviour genetics". *Annual Review of Psychology*, 39(1), 101-133.

Maddy, E. (2005) "A Review of Literature Examining Why African-Caribbean People Are More Likely to Be Diagnosed with Schizophrenia and Have a Less Desirable Access into Psychiatric System When Compared with White People Using, Systematic Approaches". (MSc Dissertation) Unpublished.

Maslow, Abraham H. (1999) "Toward a Psychology of Being (3. Ed.)". New York: Wiley. ISBN 0-471-29309-1.

McAdams, Dan P. (2009) "The person: a new introduction to personality psychology (5th ed.)". Hoboken, N.J.: Wiley. 113, 115. ISBN 978-0-470-12913-5

McLeod, S. (2007) "Abraham Maslow. Ryerson University". Retrieved August 24, 2015 fromhttp://www.ryerson.ca/~glassman/humanist. html#Maslow.

McLeod, S., (2007) "Carl Rogers. Simply Psychology". Retrieved August 21, 2015 from http://www.simplypsychology.org/carl-rogers.html.

McLeod, S. A. (2007) "Psychodynamic Approach in Psychology. Simply Psychology". Retrieved August 24 fromhttp://www.simplypsychology.org/ psychodynamic.html

McLeod, S. A. (2008). "Psychosexual Stages". Retrieved from www. simplypsychology.org/psychosexual.html

McMurran, M. (2008) "Personality Disorders, in K. Soothill, P. Rogers and M. Dolan (Eds)" *Handbook of Forensic Mental Health, Cullompton:* Willan.

Mehta, P. and Gosling, S. (2006). "How Can Animal Studies Contribute to Research on the Biological Bases of Personality"? In Canli, Turhan. Biology of personality and individual differences. Guilford Press. ISBN 1593852525.

Millon, T. and Davis, R. (1999) "Personality Disorders in Modern Life". New York: John Wiley and Sons

Mischel, W. (1993) "Behavioural conceptions". In W. Mischel, Introduction to personality New York: Harcourt Brace. 295–316

Moran, P. (1999) "Antisocial personality disorder: an epidemiological perspective". Gaskell, London

Moran, Paul (1999) "Epidemiology of personality disorders" retrieved from https://bulger.co.uk/prison/PrevelancePD.doc

Nakao, K., Gunderson, J. G., Phillips, K. A., et al (1992) "Functional impairment in personality disorders". *Journal of Personality Disorders*, 6, 24–33.

National Institute For Clinical Excellence (NICE) (2009) "Borderline Personality Disorder". London: NICE

National Institute For Mental Health In England (NIMHE) (2003a) "Personality Disorder: No Longer A Diagnosis Of Exclusion. Policy Implementation Guidance For The Development Of Services For People with Personality Disorder". London: NIMHE

Odin van der Stelt, Dounia Boubakri and Max Feltzer (2013) "Migration Status, Familial Risk for Mental Disorder, and Schizotypal Personality Traits". Department of Developmental and Clinical Psychology, Tilburg University, Tilburg, The Netherlands

O'Donohue, W., Fowler, K. A. and Lilienfield, S.O. et al (2007) "Personality Disorders: Towards the DSM-V". London: Sage

Palmer, R. (2001) "Dialectical behaviour therapy for borderline personality disorder". *Advances in Psychiatric Treatment*, 8, 10–16.

Pervin, L. A. (1993) "Personality: Theory and research". John Wiley and Sons.

Read U. and Doku V. (2012) "Mental Health Research in Ghana: A Literature Review". *Ghana Medical Journal.* Jun;46(2 Supplement)

Roychowdhury, A. and Adshead, G (2014) "Violence risk assessment as a medical intervention: ethical tensions". Psychiatric Bulletin. 38: 75–82.

Rutter, M (1979) "Maternal Deprivation, 1972-1978: New Findings, new concepts, new approaches". *Child Development,* 50, 283–305

Ryle, A. and Golynkina, K. (2000) "Effectiveness of time-limited cognitive analytic therapy of borderline personality disorder: factors associated with outcome". *British Journal of Medical Psychology,* 73, 197–210.

Schwartz, B., and Lacey, H. (1982) "Behaviourism, science, and human nature". New York: Norton.

Sher, K. and Trull, T. (1994) "Personality and Disinhibitory Psychopathology: Alcoholism and antisocial personality disorder". *Journal of Abnormal Psychology* 103:92–102.

Shields, J. (1976) "Heredity and environment. In A textbook of human psychology" 145–160. Springer. Netherlands.

Sikanartey T. and Eaton W.W. (1984) "Prevalence of schizophrenia in the Labadi district of Ghana". Acta Psychiatrica Scandinavica. 1984; 69:156–161.

Skinner, B. F. (1931) "The concept of the reflex in the description of behaviour". *Journal of General Psychology,* 5, 427–458.

Skinner, B. F. (1984a) "Operational analysis of psychological terms". *Behavioural and Brain Sciences,* 7, 511–517.

Skinner, B. F. (1984b) "Selection by consequences". *Behavioural and Brain Sciences,* 7, 477–481.

Stephanie Pappas, (2013) "Live Science Contributor" November 18, 11:38pm ET

Stoop, D. and Masteller, J. (1997) "Forgiving Our Parents, Forgiving Ourselves: Healing Adult Children of Dysfunctional Families". Regal. ISBN 978-0830734238.

Stroop, J. R. (1935) "Studies of interference in serial verbal reactions". Substance Abuse and Personality Disorders | Alcohol alcoholrehab.com/drug-addiction/substance-abuse-and-personality-disorders/ *Journal of experimental psychology,* 18(6), 643.

Sulloway, F. J. (1991) "Reassessing Freud's case histories: The social construction of psychoanalysis". *Isis,* 82(2), 245–275.

Terracciano, A. et al. (2009). "Variants of the serotonin transporter gene and NEO-PI-R Neuroticism: No association in the BLSA and Sardinia samples". *Am J Med Genet B Neuropsychiatry Genet* 150B (8): 1070–7. Doi: 10.1002/ajmg.b.30932. PMC 2788669.PMID 19199283.

The British Council (2004) "Migration, distress and cultural identity". *British Medical Bulletin,* Vol. 69

Tulving, E. (1972) "Episodic and semantic memory. In E. Tulving and W. Donaldson (Eds.), Organization of Memory". New York: Academic Press. 381–403

Watt, R. W. and Norman, F. (1981) "The abnormal personality (5th Ed.)". New York: John Wiley and Sons. ISBN 978-0-471-04599-1.

Weinberg, R. S., and Gould, D. (1999) "Personality and sport". Foundations of Sport and Exercise Psychology, 25–46.

World Health Organization (1992) *"The ICD-10 Classification of Mental and Behavioural Disorders: diagnostic criteria for research".* World Health Organization, Geneva

World Health Organization (2001) "Mental Health": A Call to Action by World Ministers.

World Health Organization (2001) "The World Health Report 2001: Mental Health, New Understanding, New Hope".

Wyrwicka, W. (1984) "Natural selection and operant behaviour". *Behavioural and Brain Sciences, 7,* 501–502.

Zuckerman, M. (2006). "Chapter 3: Biosocial Bases of Sensation Seeking". In Canli, Turhan. Biology of personality and individual differences". Guilford Press. ISBN 1593852525

Websites

www. Alcoholrehab.com

http://allpsych.com/personalitysynopsis/trait.html

Boundless. *"General Strengths and Limitations of Trait Perspectives."* *Boundless Psychology*. Boundless, 26 May. 2016. Retrieved 01 Jul. 2016 from **https:// www.boundless.com/psychology/textbooks/boundless-psychology-textbook/personality-16/trait-perspectives-on-personality-79/general-strengths-and-limitations-of-trait-perspectives-312-12847**

http://www.webmd.com/mental-health/abuse-of-prescription-drugs

Lakeman Richard © 1995 *www.testandcalc.com*

Printed in the United States
By Bookmasters